# Where Are You GOD, From 9 to 5?

# Nancy B. Barcus

# Where Are You GOD, From 9 to 5?

 L·I·F·E·S·C·A·P·E·S

Fleming H. Revell Company
Old Tappan, New Jersey

Illustrated by Roselyn B. Danner.

**Library of Congress Cataloging-in-Publication Data**

Barcus, Nancy B.
    Where are you, God, from 9 to 5.

    1. Work (Theology)—Meditations.   I. Title.
BT738.5.B37   1987         242'.68         86-31311
ISBN 0-8007-1519-5

Copyright © 1987 by Nancy B. Barcus
Published by the Fleming H. Revell Company
Old Tappan, New Jersey 07675
Printed in the United States of America

The incidents in this meditation on the world of work describe real problems and real feelings. The characters and the situations are imaginative reconstructions, rather than exact reproductions; often fiction tells the clearer truth. In every chapter I have openly shared my inner experience—the ups and downs of the workaday world and the faithfulness of the God of Scripture, whose help is both practical and eternal and whose goodness is "beyond all that we could ask or think" (*see* Ephesians 3:20).

# Contents🌿

Contents

TO my many models in the workaday world,
especially Fran, Virginia, Barbara,
Margaret, Allene,
and, of course, Jim.

# Introduction🌿

I wonder sometimes if the writer of the Psalms worked in an office. The words of those age-old Scriptures speak to our everyday working experience so keenly.

". . . I was brought low, and he helped me," we read (Psalms 116:6). And, "I sought the Lord, and he heard me, and delivered me from all my fears" (Psalms 34:4).

Our fears today may be different from those David faced when he cried out to God in the wilderness or in the middle of battle, but our emotions are surely the same: Help, Lord! For there is none to deliver me! Teach me good judgment and knowledge!

How often, in the middle of an especially hard or tiring day, we have wondered if God knew or understood our trouble. And how often, as we turned to prayer and to the Scriptures, have we discovered that the same heavenly wisdom that sustained God's people through all the ages still speaks wisely to our needs.

We are confused sometimes by people who want to force their way past us to the top, reaching for fulfillment entirely on their own. But if we have ever tasted the glitter and shallowness of so much that is called "success" today, we discover again that the Psalmist was right. All those temporary glories simply "vanish away" after a time, and those who pursued the vain hope of rising to the top without any gentleness or regard for anyone else are often disappointed and sometimes bitter, or simply bored, having nothing higher to look forward to.

We call these people "burned out." The Psalmist said of them, "Indeed, you will look for their place, but it will be no more" (*see* Job 20:9). Instead, "the meek [or gentle] . . . shall delight themselves in the abundance of peace" (Psalms 37:11). *Peace*—that is the primary promise we find in Scripture; nothing in Scripture encourages us to be shallow and self-seeking.

As we sit in our offices or stand at our stations of work, we may feel perplexed, frustrated, tempted to give up our highest longings. Yet our confidence in the God who understands our feelings and our problems can remain firm. Our faith tells us that He is there, waiting to show us "a more excellent way" (1 Corinthians 12:31).

We are promised a resource of inner strength as we seek God's highest and best—a still small voice to guide us when we turn aside to the right or to the left. As we meditate and pray and listen well, we will find that every problem that comes to us in the working world has a solution within God's timing that is far greater than anything we could ever ask or think.

If we measure our lives by the promises of God, we will learn some new and surprising things about His purposes— based on the same old and cherished truths that the Bible has always held out to us.

And why are we surprised? God's answers have not changed in this late hour of human history. The God of history and the Bible is the God of offices, workplaces, and success. As we seek out these truths, our everyday experiences reflect more and more of God's abundant provision of us.

The law of his God is in his heart; none of his steps shall slide.

Psalms 37:31

# Where Are You GOD, From 9 to 5?

# 1

Out
of Work✍

---

Nothing is lonelier than being without work. I trust God when I have money in the checking account and a regular place to be during the daytime, but I tend to fear that God has abandoned me at tough times like these.

The classified ads are depressing. The only jobs listed seem dirty, low paying, or require intolerable working hours. As I scan them, a sense of panic grips my thoughts and my fingers turn ice-cold. God has abandoned me. No matter how many times He has helped me out before, I feel He can't handle this one. Finding the perfect job for me just doesn't seem to be on His agenda.

I don't *really* believe that. I have plenty of faith when it's somebody else's problem: "God has a perfect plan for your life," I affirm. But on the day I'm sitting at home, after days on the telephone and out in the job market, knocking on doors and going through job interviews, God's promises don't seem to cover jobs.

Other times, jobs came easily to me. They were mostly teaching jobs that came through my husband's teaching contacts. We tended to be hired together as a teaching team. But once I decided on a career change that would send me striking out on my own, everything was harder. It was as if I were entering the job market for the first time, with the slim credentials of a beginner.

I had no contacts. No reputation preceded me. The support of my husband and family did not soothe my anxiety. I wanted desperately to find a job. Not just any job, but the *right* job.

Everyone who has ever been in that circumstance of actively seeking employment and meeting with frustration or unsatisfactory results knows the anxiety of it. Day passes day. Phone call after phone call leads to "Sorry, not this time." Soon there comes a sense of worthlessness.

One more rejection makes the next interview even harder. Sometimes it ushers in a downward cycle of despair, so that after a while no one even finds us attractive.

I've been all the way down that cycle. With no place to turn, I finally realized that the only way to reverse my sharp descent was to force myself to read the Scriptures. It's funny how often we resist the only thing that can help us. Opening that Bible was the last thing I wanted to do.

By an act of will, I opened the pages anyway. I read,

"Have no anxiety about anything." I skimmed the words at first, but then I realized what they were saying. ". . . In everything by prayer and supplication . . . let your requests be made known to God" (Philippians 4:6 RSV).

I'd seen the verse before, but not at a time like this. As I fixed my mind on God's providence, something happened. I'd have to call it God "verifying" Himself. It was a silent transaction, barely perceptible, but it was certain, all the same. By beginning the dialogue, I had taken the most difficult step.

". . . While they are yet speaking, I will hear," I remembered reading in the Old Testament (Isaiah 65:24).

The next day, and perhaps for several more days after that, I felt almost as low, but not quite. Through prayer, I refused to continue the downward descent.

I stood in the grocery store one day, tears ready to come, still wanting to despair. No job had come my way yet. I was still making calls and trying to believe this long waiting period would work out for the best. I said the promising words from Philippians quietly, and kept pushing my grocery cart. Despair did not overtake me that day, and it never returned as forcefully again. God's presence quietly held me firm.

We are not forgotten. On the day we least anticipate it, His answer comes. And when it comes, after we've done everything we could and prayed the believing prayer that does not see what it hopes for, we understand again that God is faithful.

Have no anxiety about anything, but in everything by prayer and supplication . . . let your requests be made know to God.

Philippians 4:6 RSV

And it shall come to pass, that before they call, I will answer; and while they are yet speaking, I will hear.

Isaiah 65:24

# 2

# Employment, at Last!

"**R**emember that job we talked about two months ago? It finally opened up."

The phone call came on a day when I was concentrating on being positive about God's will in my life. The voice at the other end was responding to my most recent "call back" to inquire about a job that had sounded like my kind of employment. The problem had been a hold up on funding, my interviewer had said. "Keep calling back, though." I took that as a positive sign. At least he didn't say, "We'll keep your application on file." I'd called back several times, because I'd been told that showing an active interest in a job made your chances of getting it more likely. Your file might move to the top of the pile every time you called. But at the same time, I'd come to believe that no manipulations of my own would suffice unless the Lord Himself were ready for the pieces to fall together. That confidence had kept me going during the interim.

The job was in an area where I could use some of my skills: writing, planning, proofreading.

"Come in on Monday."

*Monday!*

Over the past twelve weeks, I had interviewed for an insurance job, a secretarial job, a reporting job, and a word-processing job, which were among the better of several "almost" possibilities.

"We have several applicants. We'll let you know," they all had said. Some let me know, and some did not. But the news was never favorable. I was not their first choice. I would never know why—was it my age, my experience, or simply that I was "second best?"

I sat in the town library one day, refusing to sit at home and brood about my unemployment, armed with my new and positive assertion of God's concern.

Idly I listed on a notepad the attributes I sought in a job:

- Allows creativity and goal-setting
- Gives me a sense of daily contribution and challenge
- Opens up new areas and skills
- Uses my interests

I had learned from several job interviews to write out my goals. "Where do you expect to be in twenty years? What do you most want in a job?" the interviewer had asked.

I showed my husband the list that night.

"Good luck," he said. "I don't always have all that in my job."

He had a very good job. A job that seemed to fill him with energy. A job he liked. Over the past fifteen years he had been a college English teacher, a dean of a small college, and now chairman of a large English department at a major university. It was his most recent job that had brought us to this town and prompted my decision to change careers.

Though he had experienced lots of job satisfaction, I knew from close range as a listening wife that it hadn't all been easy. How could I forget? He was reminding me that work is what you make it. You add your own interest and challenge to a job. Of course it looks good to people who don't know the daily price you pay. Satisfaction doesn't come automatically. I determined to remember his words.

From beginning to end, I was without a job for twelve weeks. If you count the time before I got serious about looking—while I was settling into the house after moving—maybe it was longer than that. I would have preferred to be working much sooner, and I know that for some people, immediate employment is a necessity. I believe God knows that, too. In this case, looking back, I can see that God's slower timing was probably better than my haste.

After giving up my mind-set of despair, I occupied myself with several challenges. I put everything in the house in its place. I practiced my violin for two hours a day and made it sound better. Someone else will have a different list of projects, but with the same results—good ones.

Looking back, I can see that hardly a day was wasted. Yet had you asked me at the time, I would have told you I preferred to be at work. That's how far our wisdom takes us. I was receiving answers to my prayer, even while I thought I was waiting for them.

Unless we live in a town with a booming economy, many of us may have to pass through this frustrating time of waiting and praying and trying again, especially if we have specialized skills. Jobs are not always easy to find in middle America. If we're truly hungry, we'll take whatever is available, no matter what. But if we're searching for the "right" job, we will often need a lot of patience.

Forecasters of the future say that it may become even harder to find the "right job." They say our country is shifting from an industrial to an information economy, and that will close up many jobs, even as it opens new ones. We're in the middle of that change now. Also the salary boom is slowing down, with less chance of a sudden economic improvement.

We'll need more patience and trust than ever as these changes surround us. And we'll need even more inner peace and contentment once our newfound job begins. The wisdom of God, which is from everlasting to everlasting, will still prove to be wonderfully constant.

Today I can see that this particular job came at the right time. Not *my* right time—*God's* right time. He seems to have a lot more time than I have.

> Commit thy way unto the Lord; trust also in him; and he shall bring it to pass.
>
> Psalms 37:5

Where Are You, God?

# 3

# The "Perfect" Job ✥

The job was far from perfect. Actually there wasn't a lot to do at first. New jobs can be like that, or else they can be too hectic to get hold of. This one was slow.

When you get right down to it, I've decided, jobs are what you make of them, or what you don't make of them.

I had a nice desk, a typewriter with a correction key, and lots of paper clips and paper. The boss said, "Write me this brochure and bring it to me later this week."

I know now he hoped I'd take a long time. I'm no̲ ̲hat way. I'm a frenzied worker. I folded some paper, planned out a design, and squeezed out some good-sounding words for each page. Soon I was turning the rough draft in to him.

"Okay," he said, and set it on a pile. He fished around and handed me some material to "study over," as he called it.

I went back to my corner. When I had read it and absorbed enough of it, I filed it away and wrote a letter home. The boss would have no more ideas for me today, his look had said.

Several days passed like that. It's not that there was no work to do. Rather there was so much that nobody had time to explain in detail. It was up to me to figure it out for myself. I looked around me, noticing everyone at work, and wondered what to do.

At the next desk, Kathy was frantically using the telephone to contact some clients for information. Just twelve feet from me, she occupied another world, full and busy and self-sufficient.

Across from me, a desk was empty. Hal had been called upstairs to sit in on a conference.

I decided to try the boss one more time.

"I'm an energetic person," I said to him. "If you can just give me some idea what you need, I'll find ways to do it."

He looked happy with my offer. "I hired you because I needed another person," he said. "We have more brochures and advertising requests than we can handle, and we've got the newsletter to do, too. We're overloaded. But I'm not sure where you fit in yet."

"Let me try anything," I said. "Tell me where your worst overload is. Let me look over someone's shoulder until I catch on."

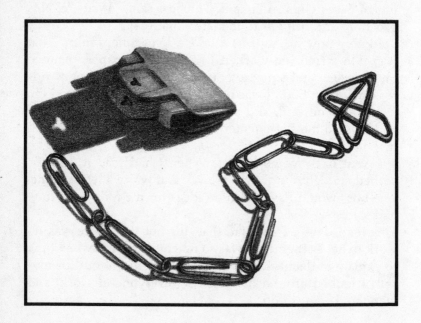

Where Are You, God?

"Sure," he said. "That's fine." I could see he was trying to be understanding. "Our problem is the newsletter. There's not enough of the right kind of information in it. I'm not sure what it needs. Give me some ideas."

It wasn't very specific. I wished he'd given me a stack of things to do. I know that happens in some jobs and you get snowed under. It's feast or famine, and either way it's tough to feel comfortable in a new job.

It's not what you'd call satisfying work, this business of trying to learn the ropes. For several months after starting a new job, any meaning we extract from life has to come from something besides the job. Until the job begins to "click," work can hardly be called satisfying. We need something other than work to see us through for a while.

Many who begin new jobs are apt to find themselves in these circumstances, since most people step into a situation that is not tailor-made for them. Whether the job description requires checking groceries through a computerized scanner, taking telephone orders, filling out insurance forms, or anything else, it's up to us to figure out how we fit in with what we find on the job. No one else can do that for us.

While that's a distinct challenge, we also may find ourselves depressed at first. The "high" of being hired soon wears off, and we must live from day to day. With God's ample help, we can do that. I was thankful for my family and for the hours I'd spent practicing my music. I returned to it in the evenings, tired as I was, and the music comforted me. I greeted the coming of green trees and lavender bluebonnets clustered on the Texas hillsides. I welcomed anything that confirmed what I could not yet see in the world of work—that life made sense and that God was in control.

When personal experiences seem temporarily bleak, God seems to use those spaces to strengthen trust and clarify the meaning of hope. Our faith is based on things we cannot yet see. Funny how those well-known passages suddenly seem to jump out of nowhere at just the right moment.

> Now faith is the substance of things hoped for, the evidence of things not seen.
>
> Hebrews 11:1

# 4

# Think Big—
# Start Small🖋

I determined, after several rounds of prayer, that I would stick it out and make this job work. After all, it's the one God gave me to do. But for one reason or another, things were just not falling into place.

During the interim, that crucial time for proving ourselves, I desperately needed some tactics that would tide me over. Today I call those methods "think big—start small."

I realized that if I could make something unique to my own interests work within the context of the office, I would be in essence rewriting my own job description and raising its interest level. I might also be able to make a contribution to the office. At the same time, I knew I had to be careful not to interfere with the established work procedures.

I have a special interest in science, which carried over from my school days. Not the highly technical kind, but a sort of curiosity about things, which I learned from my father. In our advertising work, some of the clients are also scientists. They ask us to describe their work to the general public in order to achieve certain results.

Nobody liked these assignments much, I learned, and they tended to get slighted. I began to show an interest in some of them and finally asked if I might try one.

"Sure, if you want to," Kathy said. "It's pretty dull. There's not a whole lot to work with."

"I don't mind," I said. "Let me try."

Kathy handed me the assignment. "It's something about a water purification process based on a new chemical additive." She read off the words to me. She wrinkled her nose. "Good luck," she said. And then she turned back to writing the blurb for a record jacket—something she liked better.

I called up the water-purification scientist and made an appointment, then went to see him.

"Tell me how this works," I said.

"Know any chemistry?" he asked.

"A little," I said. I didn't tell him *how* little.

He began to sketch some formulas on a paper for me, and I began to ask some questions (not enough to reveal all my shortcomings). Pretty soon we had the process down in my notebook, in very general terms. He looked satisfied.

Back at my desk I stuggled to make what I had learned sound interesting. I showed the notes to Hal, whom I expected knew a good bit more about technical things.

"Glad that's not my assignment," he said. "Chemistry is not a hot item, is it?"

I was determined that it would be.

"NECESSITY MAY BE THE MOTHER OF INVENTION, BUT THE FATHER OF INVENTION IS THE MAKER OF A NEW WATER PURIFICATION PROCESS," I typed on my blank paper.

I showed it to Hal.

"Probably the best we can do, under the circumstances," he quipped, and then added, "Not bad, really. Johnson may go for it."

The boss did indeed go for it. He liked the finished work enough to give me the next technical assignment (on an oil-drilling experiment) and then another on citrus tree grafting, for a large orchard grower.

I was still low on the office totem pole, but I'd found something that needed to be done and taken hold of it. It was a foot in the door, a toehold. When I realized the worst was over, I remembered to be thankful. God's promises had already brought me a long way and sustained me during a very bleak time.

Thinking back on it, I realize that others have done the same thing. I'll never know if prayer drove them to it or they just had more common sense than I had to begin with. I know that my best ideas come only after I've turned my dead-end despair over to God and determined to wait for Him to lead me out.

One day a new secretary started a different filing system, so things didn't get lost as easily. Her changes didn't upset anyone's routines.

Another person changed the method for keeping track of assignments, so everyone knew who was working on what. She proved herself an organizer, and no one protested a bit at her streamlined approach. She implemented it with a minimum of fanfare.

I'm sure all of us were capitalizing on God-given abilities—in my case, an old one that had never been used much before. We never suspect how something we know (or are) will turn out to serve us.

What other people did, and what I had to learn to do, was to inject some imagination into an otherwise routine setting.

If the job predictions for the next several years prove right, this approach is what more and more of us will have to do, wherever we are. More people everywhere will hold service jobs, we are told. Those are the jobs that keep our economy running—clerking, office work, data processing, and so much more. But the old upward mobility jobs will slow down, and service jobs will predominate.

If that's so, there will be many more people still to come who will desperately need the inner resources of contentment and imagination that can make their jobs "work" for them.

Probably the thing I needed most was a prayerful determination to let God help me as I sought the keys to this workaday routine. I knew my job had potential; that it was where I needed to be for my own professional growth. Knowing that, I prayed for the imagination I so sorely needed.

Yes, I think God is in the imagination business. I needed His impetus in order to feel creative again. A new freedom of spirit began to come as I realized that His "still small voice" was prompting me to live every day as creatively as I knew how, even in little ways. Jobs become what God's promptings within us make of them.

I will walk before the Lord in the land of the living.
Psalms 116:9

Where Are You, God?

# 5

Criticism🖋

---

The white paper in my work basket was covered with red writing. The note at the top said, "Try this again." Across the bottom it read, "See next page for suggestions."

My stomach tightened and my eyes glazed over. This was a project I had worked on so carefully a month ago. I had thought it was good. They had not. They had taken a long time to let me know.

On the next page was a complete revision of everything I'd done—in somebody else's style. I wanted to rumple it up and go home.

For some reason, criticism feels like a personal insult. When it comes, I freeze up and my work flow stops. If it isn't good enough, what do I do now? It is tempting to despair.

Usually there isn't another soul we can tell. After all, we don't want all the other people in the office to know we've been put down.

I've found that bearing up under criticism is one of the most demanding challenges of the office world. When it comes—sometimes several days after I've completed the work and passed on to something else—it can hit like a thunderbolt.

Recalling those times, I still tremble. It is one thing to be corrected for a deliberate misdeed. That we are likely to feel we deserve. It is quite another thing to be censured for something we didn't know was wrong—for something we tried our very best to do right. We feel helpless to change when we've already done the best we know how.

While I was trying to adapt to what those in charge wanted, I had to overcome the idea that every criticism undercut my self-esteem. My integrity as a person was not affected.

The pain of criticism often drove me to prayer. As I waited for moments of calm to overtake me, I slowly began to see that my standing with God was entirely unchanged by what someone thought of my work.

My personal security was solely a matter between God and me. It was something He had given His word on. Nothing could change His care for me. "None shall ever pluck them out of my hand" (*see* John 10:28).

I remember another phrase, which had never seemed so pointed as now. "Nothing shall separate us from the love of Christ" (*see* Romans 8:38, 39). Paul offered a list of calamities far more horrendous than a rejected piece of paper.

God's promises and my situation in His providence and care were unchanged. He was not displeased with me because of my ups and downs at work.

When I was able to think more objectively, I also realized that every difficulty moved me toward something greater in terms of skill and efficiency. God was probably using these times to stretch my inner wisdom in some way, maybe teaching me not to think of myself more highly than I ought to think, but with sober judgment (*see* Romans 12:3). I learned to believe that no experience, pleasant or not, is wasted. He is doing something I cannot yet understand. The only way to learn may sometimes be by a jolt or two. I've reminded myself of that many times.

Within a few weeks I caught on to what was required and gradually came up with work that was on target more often than not. Maybe that first criticism could have been a little more tactful, but we aren't allowed the privilege of selecting a preferred style for the delivery of criticism.

Some of us are just too sensitive, no matter how kindly we are approached. I know I am.

> . . . God is faithful, who will not suffer you to be tempted above that ye are able; but will with the temptation also make a way to escape, that ye may be able to bear it.
> 1 Corinthians 10:13

# 6

# Waiting
# Your Turn🖋

"I think we should. . . ."

My voice was charged with excitement. I had a good idea.

I saw the frown. The words died in my throat. The idea would have to wait.

Six weeks is too soon to have a better idea.

In every office, the waiting time is different. Some employers say they want you to "hit the ground running," but they don't mean hit the ground running in a different direction. Sometimes new ideas—really good ones—require a radical change of direction. Building up the credibility to suggest wide-ranging changes takes time.

Patience, of course, is the last thing we want to exercise when we have a good idea. Usually our ideas seem so good that we want them to happen *now*. Things could be so much better, if only they'd try it. But they won't.

"There are people here who think you're too aggressive—pushing too fast." My boss was trying to be tactful, I could see. He was repeating the words to me after I asked him why an idea I'd turned out had come back with a note attached that said, "We can't do it this way. Check our guidelines for standard procedure."

I had tried something different. After just a few weeks, I was already weary of the same old way everyone seemed to do things. I thought the office needed some changes.

"Why can't we do this?" I asked. "I think it would help. It would give us some new information for the newsletter. People would like it."

"How do you know?"

"I've been asking around. People who read the newsletter say they'd like to read about the professional seminars we have here—in case they can't get to them."

He stared at me coldly. "When it's time for outside opinions," he said, "I'll get those."

"Sure," I said. "All right."

I stepped back toward the door. I wanted to defend my idea. I had thought a long time about it. Every week a visiting expert came in to discuss the latest market trends, or the psychology of management, or something else that interested me. I thought we should report it in the newsletter.

"People would read the newsletter instead of just throwing it away, if we had things like this in it," I said. "I'm just sure of it." As I said the words, I heard the implied insult. It was too late to retract the words now.

"Don't be so aggressive," Mr. Johnson said to me.

I blanched. *Aggressive? Mr. Johnson has been reading too many articles on women in the work force,* I thought. "I'm just trying to do a good job," I said. "I'm not trying to be aggressive."

I wondered if I should cry. I felt like it, but it would seem like cheating to use tears on him. I knew my face was very red and tight.

"I know you're trying to do good work," he said. His voice softened. "Maybe we'll try your idea sometime. But next time you have a good idea, come and talk with me first, before you let it out all over the office."

I nodded.

"I don't like surprises," he added.

"Okay," I said. And I left.

I still thought my idea was a good one. As a matter of fact, the office did eventually try it, with good results.

But I could see my timing had been all wrong, as had my

tactics. I had not been listening very carefully for the still small voice. This was a project I'd thought up all by myself, in great haste. I hadn't taken time to consider its impact. Had I run the idea through a quiet space of prayer, I might have seen from the first that I was being hasty.

Good ideas happen slowly. The people who approve and implement them have to feel they are involved in the change. They have to feel they were not ignored or railroaded into doing something before they were convinced of it themselves. Bosses, especially, have to feel that an idea's success was because of, and not in spite of, their opinion. I wish I had known that *before* I rushed ahead. I suppose God Himself might have restrained me, had I given Him the chance.

To make changes and still maintain office harmony takes longer than simply making the changes without regard to other people. It takes a while to build up confidence among office colleagues so an idea will be accepted. Good ideas at

the wrong time are resented. That, of course, is the voice of experience talking—call it hindsight.

I still think that if I had been less hasty, more reponsive to the still small voice in an attitude of prayer, I would have handled things better, even without knowing all I eventually learned the hard way.

Now I remind myself, "Why waste a good idea by being in a hurry?"

> . . . Add to your faith . . . temperance; and to temperance patience. . . .
>
> 2 Peter 1:5, 6

Where Are You, God?

# 7

# Recovering
# From Mistakes🌿

The angry voice on the other end of the phone said, "You've made a terrible mistake. What are you going to do about it?"

"Who is this?" I asked, trembling.

"Dr. Green," the caller said. "I asked you to change the information on the statistical charts. I saw the material today, and you didn't change anything. You've made me look very bad."

I searched for the right words. "I'm sorry," I said.

"That's not good enough," he told me.

I fished the chart from my drawer. I hadn't noticed the mistakes. I looked at it while he talked. He was right.

I told him I would call him right back, and I hung up. I wanted to think about how it had happened.

It was probably the worst mistake I had made so far. I had just gotten back to work from a day's illness and was feeling a little rocky. Things like this usually hit when you're least mentally prepared, I've found.

I closed my eyes and tried to recollect. Dr. Green had requested the changes the day before deadline. We'd had four more items to finish and another immediate request from the president of the company that same day.

I passed the changes on to a colleague and never checked back to be sure they had gotten into the chart. It wasn't directly my fault, but it was my fault, too, because I should have made certain before letting the item go onto the press.

I would have to tell Dr. Green it was my fault. I dialed the phone.

When people are angry, my instincts say to avoid them. But in a case like this, we have to take our medicine.

"We'll print a correction," I said.

"That won't help," he said. "The damage is done."

"We'll print it anyway," I said. "We really want to help, Dr. Green. Please let us try to make it right."

"Well, all right," he said sternly, and he hung up.

The retraction wouldn't change the mistake. The man probably had been wronged by my error. Mistakes are frightening. They affect more than ourselves, sometimes in a ripple effect. The temptation is to find someone else to blame for them. In this case I could have pointed a finger at someone else. In other cases, I can often find and claim some extenuating circumstances. It's tempting to use all the means at our disposal to salvage our image.

We reason that others have used these same means to implicate us in *their* mistakes, but it's not fair, whether we do it or they do. And it doesn't change the error. Nor does it promote long-term good feeling in the office. If I take it on the chin this time, maybe someone else will take in on the chin for me next time.

At any stage—but especially when we're still gaining confidence about the details of our job or about acceptance among peers—facing up to mistakes can feel very life threatening.

Fortunately, prayerful afterthought reminded me that my error did not in any way affect my relationship with God. "I will never leave thee, nor forsake thee," He says (Hebrews 13:5).

I may have committed a tactical error, but I had not sinned. More than that, I tried to handle the situation with a clear conscience, rather than implicating others in my mistake. That acceptance of blame may have made some others in the office think less of me, but God cares more about attitudes. He thinks better of me for my frank acceptance of blame.

It's easy to forget that He is as much in control of our professional lives as of our personal lives, working according to the same biblical principles that guide our relationships with family and friends. Why is that so hard to remember?

True, He doesn't promise me that I will never make another mistake. But I can rest secure that God's attitude toward me remains the same. "Walk in the light," He says. If I am careful to do that, He will see me through with the rest.

Wait on the Lord: be of good courage, and he shall strengthen thine heart. . . .

Psalms 27:14

# 8

Pecking
Order

"I wish they'd ask me to do it," I said to myself under my breath. I was overhearing a phone conversation, and I knew more about the background of the inquiry than the person answering the telephone.

I wasn't expected to take phone inquiries. Speaking to the public was a job for seasoned veterans. My turn would come later, when I knew more. That was the structure of things.

When you're the last one hired, it doesn't matter what you already know. Prior experience doesn't count—especially when it is prior experience of another kind. The office can be a bit like the military: Rank is everything.

People feel comfortable with well-defined pecking orders. They like to keep the order in place, especially when they've got the upper berth. It's a situation that's hard to change—except through waiting.

As I sat at my desk, watching others assume responsibility while I waited my turn, it was hard to think that God is not concerned with my status, and not in a hurry. If I wanted advancement so much, surely He must want it more, I reasoned.

I've since decided that what He prefers is a steady upward direction that is not too fast for Him to do His work in His more perfect way. God doesn't ride roughshod over others for His own advantage, so He isn't likely to do it for me, either.

Waiting for something to change, I swallowed my frustration and determined to let God do things His way. In the meantime, I would just have to look for whatever spice and interest I could bring to my present assignments.

The longtime people in our office have weathered similar crises and hung on. They can repeat stories to me of surprising insensitivity—things that hurt them far more than the little slights I've felt. The worst thing that can happen to you, they say, is to be pigeonholed, stuck in a slot. "That's her job. We don't do that," is the way it goes. Pigeonholing ranges from such little things as who picks up the huge sack of mail in the morning and trudges back for five bulky newspapers, to who is left out of an office lunch invitation because their views "don't count."

The message from those little incidents is that you're an insignificant person in the scheme of things, and are likely to stay that way. I've seen the hurt expressions after some of these things, and it hurts me, too.

I've heard such offhand explanations as, "She's only a secretary," with all the lack of esteem implied in that statement. I've seen the disappointment of those left behind in the office while some of us went off to cover special assignments.

Some of that was my lot at first, so I know exactly how it feels. I'd sit there and watch the others move about freely with all their privilege and self-assurance. They never felt the need to explain their doings or draw me into them. It would have helped so much if I could have felt included in the enterprise or could have shared the feeling that their success was important to the entire office community.

I think that's all anyone really wants—to feel included or needed at whatever level the work is assigned. After all, unless everybody contributes, everything stops, from typists and mail carriers to all the rest. That sense of contribution carries with it an attitude of confidence and hope.

But we can't always have it that way. Sometimes we have to live with the slights. We can't *make* people be sensitive. That's where our inner relationship with God comes in. No matter what, He is our source of strength and confidence. More than that, He can work through circumstances as we pray, to make them more tolerable for us and to change our painful reactions to them.

No, I certainly don't think God would ask me to survive in truly intolerable situations. At least not under normal circumstances. (History, of course, has proved that He can provide the strength for anything.)

But I see now that God has His own timing.

Were I never to be promoted at all, I'd have to believe that with God's help, I could discover still more innovative ways to do my work.

> Therefore being justified by faith, we have peace with God through our Lord Jesus Christ . . . And not only so, but we glory in tribulations also: knowing that tribulation worketh patience; And patience, experience; and experience, hope.
>
> Romans 5:1, 3, 4

# 9            Queen Bee

Every office has had at least one. She's been in and out of my office a few times, too. I've heard tales of her from others who know her well.

She's fiercely protective of the boss and of any access to him. She's secretive about the chief priorities of the office; she's determined to keep everyone else on the other side of the fence.

If you go to her with a request that begins, "Mr Johnson sent me to ask you if you would . . ." she frowns. Mr. Johnson didn't tell *her* to do it. She doesn't take orders, except from him.

"We don't usually do that," she says. "Give the memo with your suggestion to me." She lays it on a pile, and you know she'll never pass it on or do it unless he tells her directly. The memo will still be there, unfiled and unhandled, in six weeks.

"Can you help me with this?" I asked her another day, handing her a project I'm working on. It needs a few details that only she knows how to locate.

She takes it from me, makes a few marks on it, and lays it aside, nodding. As I go out, I see her putting more marks on it.

The next day, I see it on Mr. Johnson's desk. He tells me she thought it needed a lot of work. Why didn't she tell me?

It isn't nice to be suspicious, but I think it's her way of keeping me under control. I'm not the only one in the office whose work she's secretly exposed to the boss. She never shows him the best things.

Most of the queen bees I know are women. That is probably because I am a woman, and queen bees tend to annoy their own sex. The fact is, I've heard men confess to their own special type of queen bee. I've heard them tell stories of getting in one another's way to prevent a promotion. I've heard them accuse one of their group of being excessively bossy or abusive. I don't know everything about the male "queen bee," but I don't believe the stereotype applies exclusively to women. Getting along in a competitive world brings out a multitude of problems and bad tactics. No one seems to want anyone else to get ahead. Strange, isn't it?

The queen bee in the next office to mine has some of these feelings, I'm sure. She's vivacious on the telephone, friendly to visitors to the office, but the lines around her desk are firmly drawn. If someone has a problem in the next area, it's none of her concern. If there's a personal problem or a slip-up involving her, she assumes it's someone else's fault, and she never forgets it. You can tell she's making a mental list because when a certain person's name is mentioned, her lips purse up with disapproval.

As long as the queen bee reigns in the office, I'm told, you might as well forget about any restructuring that will improve your status. She likes things the way they are, or better yet, the way they *were*. It's up to you to like it or *leave*.

In dealing with her, you can take several tacks. The situation is not completely beyond your control.

The most obvious tack is to leave or ask for a transfer. I know people who have done that. Their sense of dread as they approached the office unpleasantness each morning grew like a cloud, and their mental health settled the matter. The queen bee would never change, so their withdrawal was the only way to regain sanity, they reasoned.

Facing the queen bee head-on to resolve the differences is

an approach others have tried, but with mixed results. Approaching her with the best will in the world to discuss problems or feelings may elicit open amazement on her part. "Why, I never meant to give you that impression," she says. "I'm not aware of any problem at all." Her eyes reflect a blank. She does not know what you mean.

Does she or doesn't she? There are days when her motives seem pointed and dark. But it is possible she is using a defense mechanism that has been so long a part of her personality that she is truly unaware of it.

Praying for God's objectivity seems impossible when we are hurting from her slights. But in a moment of calm and a season of prayer, I have seen several things. She may be an unhappy person, without warm or fulfilling relationships in her home. She may feel insecure about her abilities or the rank to which life seems to have assigned her. If so, putting up barriers is her only means of protection for the fragile hold she has on her inner life. No matter whether her personality is loud and overbearing or quiet and tense, her inner self may be aflutter with anxiety.

It's likely she does not know herself well enough to have sorted these things out. Whatever it feels like to be the way she is, she is so used to it that she can't even consider being any different.

Sometimes she makes me so angry that I find it hard to pray. That's probably when I most need to. Besides, Jesus requires it. Through prayer, I may even gain a special sensitivity to her unspoken needs. The Holy Spirit is capable of this. After a while, several things happen:

I don't mind her so much, and even grow to understand and empathize with her. With amazement, I recognize the still small voice of God prompting me to be patient with her.

My own insecurities, which she intensifies, encounter healing as I pray. When she brings me close to tears with one of her tactics, I find myself supported by an unseen protector—God's provision of the Spirit.

God's quiet working in both of us will make life in the office at least tolerable, and probably much better than that. Hers is not a problem I can solve all alone. The queen bee has been the way she is for too long.

Introducing the ingredient of prayer and the habit of reacting to her slights with quick inner prayer for God's sustenance, I find that she no longer affects me as she did.

It seems unlikely most of the time, but she may even become a friend. I can testify to that. It's happened more than once.

Our lives are founded on great promises.

Therefore ... put on tender mercies, kindness, humbleness of mind, meekness, longsuffering; bearing with one another, and forgiving one another, if anyone has a complaint against another; even as Christ forgave you, so you also must do.

Colossians 3:12, 13 NKJV

Where Are You, God?

# 10

I've been overlooked for an interesting assignment, and I feel bitter about it.

I suspect that someone staying after hours and getting a pat on the back for it is just trying to impress the boss. I couldn't stay, even if I wanted to. At home four people are waiting for me.

I wonder why a promotion went to someone whose tactics seem so much like blatant apple polishing.

If I could just let it all out to someone, I'd feel so much better. Psychlogists say we need to vent our anger. Doctors say bottling things up causes ulcers. The danger we face, though, is venting our feelings in the wrong place.

The worst place in the world is within the office. Every negative word says as much about ourselves as it does about others. Worse than that, it places our colleagues in the uncomfortable position of having to take sides. My complaints would destroy the quality of our teamwork.

The best place to spill feelings is outside the office.

My husband can usually see my anger coming before I even say a word. I'm unusually quiet when I first arrive home, waiting for the kids to disappear. Unless it's so urgent I can't wait. "I can't believe it," I say finally. "It happened again."

"Really?" He has learned to say only the minimum.

"Yes. Just before noon the phone rang, and when I was halfway through the call, she interrupted me and took over.

" 'I know about that,' she told me. 'Let me handle it.' "

My husband looks sorry for me.

"And that afternoon, she went to Mr. Johnson and let him know how well she had handled everything. I had already done all the paperwork, and when she turned in her report, she put her name on everything. She writes these long reports about all the wonderful things she does and keeps turning them in to him."

He's still listening and not saying a word. He used to try to make me feel better. Now he knows his only job is to listen until I've got it said.

"It's awful," I say.

He nods.

I want to say something really mean about her, but I've learned to be angry about actions and not about people. Somehow when I verge on saying something really hateful, my stomach tightens, and I know I need to stop. There's a difference between hate and anger. The still small voice usually gives me an immediate clue when I've gone too far. "Call not thy brother a fool," the Bible says (*see* Matthew 5:22).

"Things will get better," my husband says. And then he stops, wondering if he has said too much. I don't need consolation or cheering up. There is nothing he is expected to say to me. I just want him to listen. I just need to know that my words have been heard. And that's the end of it. Until next time.

Between now and then, though, maybe he'll need me to do the same for him. The secret in the exchange is genuine listening, without anything else required.

Even if I had no one else to listen to my complaint, I still have that heavenly advocate who knows more than we ask or think. God hears even as we are yet speaking. He sorts out the anger and hurt, then He soothes and mends.

Prayer—that literal, word-by-word pouring out to God all our hurt and complaint—relieves the pent up anger that churns and damages our spirit. When psychologists say we need to vent our anger, I suspect some of them never thought of prayer as a place to do such a thing. Actually forming the words, verbalizing point for point what is bothering us, takes that great unformed mass of trouble and reduces it to size. The act of prayer is the beginning of healing.

That doesn't mean that when I get to my feet again everything will be solved. That doesn't seem to be the way God answers prayer. But I am no longer carrying the sting. Naming a hurt aloud to someone—a friend, a spouse, or God Himself—frees us from its threat.

The rest is up to God. In His own time, He will ease the pain. One day I will wake up in the morning and not even remember why I was angry.

> I cried unto the Lord with my voice. . . . I poured out my complaint before him; I shewed before him my trouble. When my spirit was overwhelmed within me, then thou knewest my path. . . .
>
> Psalms 142:1–3

# 11

# A Sense
of Balance

"**Y**ou're not listening."

I stared across my plate, barely hearing. I was trying to figure out what would happen to the child-welfare system in our town if some legislation the office was promoting did not pass.

"Nancy?"

It was hard to come back to the conversation at the dinner table. My mind had been working all day on the facts and figures of child care. I wanted to choose just the right angle for my blurb on it.

"Let's take a walk tonight. It's such a warm evening. All the bluebonnets are out."

"Sure," I said. I tried to smile.

"How was your day?" my husband asked.

I felt I should have asked him about his. I was struggling hard to come back to the moment at hand. It was hard to let go of my own day. "Fine," I said. "How was yours?"

"Fine," he said, and little else, sensing my distraction. "Now tell me what's on your mind."

I shrugged my shoulders. I couldn't talk about all the facts swirling through my head. I was afraid the phone would ring, or someone would interrupt me. I knew that once I started to talk, it would be a long, long story.

We started our walk after supper in silence. The steady

A Sense of Balance                                                    55 crunch of our feet on the gravel underfoot soothed and quieted me. Finally I said, "My mind is just whirling. I've got to calm down. This child-welfare project has jammed my thinking processes."

"I wondered what it was," he said. "You're so far away."

"It's because it's all so interesting," I said, surprising myself at the admission after so many months. "I just can't let go of it tonight."

"My mind is off somewhere, too," my husband said.

His words brought me back. I hadn't even noticed. "Really?"

He could see I was surprised. "Yes," he said. "Jones is quitting the faculty. He's so vocal about his dissatisfaction, it means there's probably a fight brewing. I'm afraid of what will happen to the linguistics program now."

The news hit me hard. My husband had been worried about something much closer to his everyday life. And tonight he'd sat there at the dinner table, probably wanting to talk about it, and I'd been too preoccupied to notice. "Tell me about it," I said. I forced my thoughts back to listen. We walked for a long time while he talked.

When he finally finished, we stood a minute, then turned to start back.

"It really helps to talk to someone," he said.

"I know," I said. We were silent a minute. My mind was still full, and I forced the fullness back.

"Lord, help," I prayed as we walked. "Do something about my racing thoughts."

I didn't even know what that might be. I only knew I had lost my perspective. My little project at work was fascinating indeed, but it was not going to make that much difference. The burden for passing the legislation was in other hands. I was only interested in doing a great job with the publicity.

Whether it was child welfare or an airplane that flies on

fuel from candy bars, I was beginning to attach too much importance to my work. Now that things were going well, I was beginning to lose my sense of balance.

"What about your day?" my husband said quietly. "That's enough about mine."

"It was a good one, again," I said. "But I just can't get it out of my mind. The really interesting things at work are starting to go round and round in my head."

"I've had that happen," he said. "I finally had to learn to pace myself. When I feel it start to happen, I step away from it, if I can."

There was a time when I wished I could have given him that very advice. He'd learned it himself, probably from the Giver of all wisdom. He used to be so involved in his own world that he was unable to talk to me. Somehow he'd learned to set it all aside at the end of most days, especially when one of us needed him. I wondered just how he had managed to do it.

"The voice of experience talking," I said. "How did you do it?"

"I learned it the hard way," he said. "Wish I could give you a shortcut."

"Just knowing it doesn't have to be this way is a help," I said. "You can switch your mind on and off most of the time, can't you?"

"Most," he said. "At least, better than I used to do."

I was thankful for the healing power of time. ". . . Ask, and ye shall receive . . ." the Scriptures promise (John 16:24). ". . . No good thing will he withold from them that walk uprightly" (Psalms 84:11). The words were reassuring.

I felt the pressure in my mind ease.

The evening winds slapped at our faces and the lights began to go on in the houses as we passed. At home there would be phone calls to return, and maybe some math homework to supervise.

A Sense of Balance                                                          57

If so, we needed clear minds more than anything else.

We headed into the house, and the whirling of my mind calmed, as I recalled an old promise. . . .

The peace of God, which passeth all understanding, shall keep your hearts and minds through Christ Jesus.

Philippians 4:7

Where Are You, God?

# 12

## Work
## as Identity

"**I** can't believe they didn't like my idea," I sighed, as I sat down at the supper table. "I've spent so many hours working on it. When I was all done, someone else changed it all at our meeting."

I knew my face was ashen. I'd been looking sick for the last three hours, the mirror told me.

"That work is getting to you again," my husband said. "I hate to see you let it happen."

"But I spent so much time on it. It's a part of me," I said.

"You've put your finger right on it," he answered. "You're making that job your whole life."

"Yes," I said slowly. "It's getting to be my whole life. It makes me feel good to do something well."

"Of course it does," he said. "But if pleasing people is the basis for your view of yourself, who are you?"

He looked very serious.

"I don't know," I answered slowly, and my answer frightened me. I realized that my great anxiety about this job was based on a fear that failure would bring me all the way down. If the job didn't work for me, I was nobody.

"How old are you?" my husband asked me.

"You know how old," I said. "Too old to be starting over every day wondering who I am."

"That's the point," he said. "I've known you a long time

now. You're the same person. You have interests, sensitivities, talents, just as you've always had. Those things are the real you. Have you forgotten all that?"

Yes, I had. I had assumed that I had to keep proving myself in order to accept myself. I had assumed that I was nobody unless I was succeeding. I had come to believe that achievement in the eyes of others was everything, and that without it I was no longer the person I had been.

"You're on dangerous ground," my husband said. "You could collapse if you feel you're only a reflection of how others are feeling at the moment. You're more than that. You're everything you ever dreamed, thought, learned, believed." He stopped. "I'm surprised I'd have to be telling you this," he said.

I pushed back my chair and nodded slowly, resting my chin in my hand.

The children had left the table without saying a word, sensing that something serious was underway.

I shut my eyes. The years of ideals and impressions and convictions I'd built as scaffolding flooded in on me. Everything was still in place; a larger vision at the back of my mind still urged me forward.

But there was more. Behind it all came a voice I'd learned to hear in my teens, a still small voice that without a sound had said so often to me, "This is the way. Walk ye in it."

It was the voice that went with a vision of God Himself, in the flesh as Jesus Christ, setting aside everything on my behalf.

It was the voice that had said to me, "Will ye also go away?" And I had replied with Peter and all the rest, "I have believed, and am sure . . ." (*see* John 6:67–69).

Since first hearing that voice, I had known who I was with a finality that it seemed nothing would ever shake—not ". . . death, nor life nor angels, nor principalities, nor powers, nor things present, nor things to come," were the words I had believed (Romans 8:38).

How, indeed, could I have tied my sense of well-being into anything less?

I looked out across the hills behind the house, standing so steadily through all the winds of spring and fall, year after year. They were battered by the winds, but essentially unchanged.

I nodded.

"I've forgotten a lot," I whispered.

> Who shall separate us from the love of Christ? . . .
>
> Romans 8:35

# 13 Transcendent Help on a "Down" Day

T he clock said three minutes past five—the end of a long day. All around me, people were turning off electric typewriters, closing desk drawers with a final bang, and heading home. I was too depressed to even stand up. Today I felt I was getting nowhere.

"How long, O Lord?" I wondered, praying at the back of my mind, the way I knew David so often did in the Psalms. As my mind drifted, I remembered an old friend. She had worked in the office world for years, and had progressed from being a secretary to personnel manager of a very large pharmaceutical firm.

I wondered how she had kept her head clear all those years. Suddenly I wanted to hear her voice.

I picked up the phone, called information, and heard the phone ringing through to her at last. I tensed, wondering what she would say, hearing from me so suddenly today.

"Fran?" I said, when her voice finally came on the line. "It's Nancy, calling from Texas."

"Nancy? Really?" I could hear the warmth in her voice. I hadn't seen her in three years, but all the time between us melted away as she said my name. As I realized how close she seemed, I wondered how many of my friends had at least one person like this somewhere in the world—someone they could turn to when things weren't all they should be.

"Hold on," Fran said. "I've got someone here. Let me finish, and I'll be back to you in a second."

"Sure," I said. "Go ahead."

I was asking a lot to expect a busy executive to drop everything and talk to me. But her voice sounded welcoming, so I waited.

Finally she came back on the line.

"There," she said. "I've got my phone lines all transferred out to the main desk, so we won't be interrupted. Now, tell me how you are, Nancy." She sounded sincerely interested.

"That's what I'm calling about," I said. "I don't know how I am, Fran. I wanted to hear your voice again. I used to think I wanted to work in an office. I thought the challenge would be a good idea. But there are so many ups and downs here, Fran. Sometimes I just don't know who I am or what I'm doing here at all. I just thought maybe you could give me some good advice."

Where Are You, God?

I paused to catch my breath, wondering at my long, urgent speech.

"Advice?" I heard her voice sounding almost amused, but still very warm and personal. Fran was one of those people whose home was always open to friends and whose words were always seasoned with the grace of her deeply personal faith in Christ. I was confident she would have some insight for me. Her warmth and concern for other people had slowly inched her through the office ranks of a major corporation.

"It's not easy, is it?" she said. "I'm not sure I have any advice, Nancy. It's not an ideal world, is it? This office life?"

She sounded so lighthearted as she said it. I wondered what hardships she had overcome to sound so detached, as if she were floating above it all.

"You sound so cheerful, Fran," I said. "What's your secret? That's what I called to ask. I won't bore you with the details of what's wrong here. It's just that things bother me so much some days. I just don't feel as if I have a hold on my life the way I'd like. All the ups and downs get to me and pull me down."

"I know," Fran said. "I know."

That's all she said.

I waited.

"Fran?" I said. "Tell me what to do."

"Nancy, I'm afraid what I have to say will sound so obvious, you'll wonder why you called to hear me say it. It's the same thing we've said to each other all these years since we first met. You've been gone from the area more than ten years. I've had three title changes and moved through four different offices, and handled a lot of personnel problems— more than you want to know about. But I don't have more or less wisdom than we first shared when you came to my Bible study so many years ago."

I remembered that time. Fran's face always softened as

she talked about "the Lord Jesus and all He has done for us." I don't even remember any specific Bible passage she was teaching from, there were so many. I only remember her absolute confidence that this great Lord was sufficient for everything.

I had seen, over the doorway in her home, a hand-lettered Bible text that everyone who came there noticed right away. "Thou remainest," it said. It was a verse from the book of Hebrews, echoed from the Old Testament. Everything in the world can shift or change or die, said the Scripture, except for God Himself. He remains.

"Nancy," Fran said. "It's only the Lord Jesus who makes any difference, isn't it? Our problems change, but we're never promised we'll be free of them. It isn't reasonable to expect that of this life. People and problems come and go, but our Lord is still the same. You know that."

"Yes," I said, "but I needed to hear *you* say it."

If I were still in her office and we had two hours to talk, Fran would tell me some of the problems she had surmounted during the years, and she would listen to mine. But when we were all done, we'd be right back to what she had said across hundreds of miles of electronic signals: Jesus Christ, the same yesterday, today, and forever.

"Fran," I said, "you sound so cheerful, like you're riding above all the problems."

"It's been a rough day here, love," Fran said. "I'll be glad to get home tonight and put it all behind me. But I know, through it all—and you know it, too—that our life is rooted in the Lord Jesus. Nothing during a day's work can change that fact. If I still sound cheerful to you at this hour, that's why."

"That's what I called to hear," I said.

We didn't promise to write, and I didn't know when I would see her again. We were miles away and had no plans to visit. But her confidence in the unchanging God, sup-

Where Are You, God?

porting her as He supported me, seemed to transcend the passage of days and of time itself.

... That ye, being rooted and grounded in love, May be able to comprehend with all saints what is the breadth, and length, and depth, and height; And to know the love of Christ, which passeth knowledge. . . .

Ephesians 3:17–19

# 14

One day it occurred to me that things at work had smoothed into a steadier routine; the bumps were smaller and easier to ride out. Either you like the job by now, or you've turned in your resignation, I realized. This job was going to be permanent.

I'm not sure when that day came. I was only glad to realize that in the normal course of things there comes such a day. I recognized its coming because people in the office asked for my opinion more readily, and clients began to ask for me.

No, this wasn't the "job of my dreams" yet. *Do people really have those?* I wondered. I didn't care about that now. I cared most of all that I felt needed and that I felt competent to do the work that came my way.

I reflected that I had met some interesting people, learned several new skills, and was talking less at home about problems.

I've tried to analyze how this came about and why things finally fell into shape.

For one thing, I began to distinguish between ideals—those things we picture when we think about a particular job—and realities—the actual mixture of good and less than good circumstances that make up the everyday working world.

Most of us have no illusions about the everyday world when it comes to our families. We exchange the ideal family for the real one, once we've had some children of our own. While we think each child is wonderful, we know so well how much farther each one (and ourselves as well) has yet to go in learning to love and care for one another. There are things we would change if we could. So we pray and wait patiently, seeing slow and joyful progress in all of us.

Why is it such a surprise that the working world, which is also a mixture of personalities and problems, is no different than our family world? At home or at work, storm clouds can come up almost without warning, pour down on us unexpectedly, and then pass on. Each time, we pray and recover from the little storms of circumstance or personality. As we do, we find God ever faithful to heal and to mend.

Transferring that personal habit of realism and daily trust to the working world is a necessity, I finally understood. I learned to exchange my false expectations for realistic ones. Work, like life, has its ups and downs. But God is a constant presence through it all.

As my focus changed, I also found the demands of the job becoming second nature. Every day offered just enough variety to keep me going and presented me with something else I still needed to improve.

This greater ease about the day-to-day details ended my sense of feeling "on parade" or having to prove myself. I would always have a lot to learn, always find something else up ahead. So does everyone.

I began to feel less anxious about criticism. I had survived enough ups and downs to feel reasonably confident that my world was not about to fall apart. That confidence was increasingly undergirded as I read in the Psalms that God is an ever-present help in trouble, a refuge and strength, so that I need not fear, though the waters roar and be troubled.

Somehow I didn't mind being at the bottom, middle, or wherever I was on the totem pole. I had learned a lot of things from scratch that I'd never have learned otherwise, and never have to learn again. But there would be a lot more things still ahead to learn, and I'd feel less threatened by them, whatever they were. It's all right not to know something, I discovered.

I stopped needing to impress anybody and learned to accept myself and my job. By exchanging idealism for realism, learning to relax and accept myself and my circumstances, I began to look forward to each day.

There's an old saying: "Let go, and let God." I don't know who made it up. Funny, but that's exactly what it took for me to find contentment.

Now may the Lord of peace Himself give you peace always in every way. The Lord be with you all.
2 Thessalonians 3:16 NKJV

# 15

"Guess what JoAnn is doing right now!"

I could guess, but I didn't want to. JoAnn had taken a lot of time off lately, and it didn't appear to be for "professional reasons."

At first no one wanted to say much about it, so we all politely ignored the whole thing.

"Where's JoAnn?" someone would say.

"Out for the morning," the receptionist answered, and that was that.

JoAnn was a friendly person, new to the office, and one of those people who wasn't afraid of anything. She'd speak up in a meeting whether it was her turn or not, and follow the boss down the hall afterwards with one more "better idea."

I'd never have survived, had I used her tactics. But JoAnn was one of those people who could break all the rules and still get a smile from the people who counted. That's probably because she got her work done on deadline, so it was hard for anyone to complain.

When JoAnn was around, the tempo of the office seemed to skip just one beat faster.

So we noticed her absence when she started coming in late, or called in to say she had to see a client on the way to work—a client who apparently took most of the morning.

When she arrived in the office, she always made a big

splash, talking about how much she had accomplished and how she had persuaded the person to let her do some extra promotional material. Mr. Johnson liked that. That's probably why he never questioned her long absences, at least not at first.

But after a while it began to look as though those extra business promises were not materializing. JoAnn began to look tired, and her good-natured chatter began to break down.

One day I transferred a phone call to her. I heard her turn down a client's request in short order. The caller phoned right back to complain, and the receptionist and Mr. Johnson were both brought in on the situation.

"What's the matter with JoAnn?" Mr. Johnson asked me that afternoon. "We've had some complaints about her."

"I don't know," I said. "Why?"

"I'm not sure why," he said. "She does good work. Maybe she's just had a bad day."

I nodded. Maybe she had.

But the pattern continued. JoAnn came in late at least once a week, looking very tired. She went straight to her desk, threw her briefcase down on it, then began banging on her typewriter. No one wanted to talk to JoAnn on those days. She might reply and she might not. I noticed that people walked by her without stopping to talk at all.

*Funny*, I thought, *how a personality can change so fast when there's something wrong.*

One day a call came in to the office for JoAnn. The caller asked a lot of personal questions and then hung up. It was one of JoAnn's late mornings. Two or three of us were standing around when the call came in, so we heard the receptionist trying to be tactful.

"JoAnn's done it now," Hal finally said aloud. His comment was the first thing anybody had said on the subject.

Kathy nodded her head.

Where Are You, God?

That was the first spoken recognition of the problem, and it came as a relief after so many weeks of avoiding the obvious. Suddenly the three of us felt drawn into the secret.

It was hard, once we had acknowledged the problem, to draw back again as if there were nothing to know. Now, whenever some new development involving JoAnn occurred, we seemed to be a part of it. Lifted eyebrows and knowing glances were our way of delaying a conversation until we were alone.

Soon it was easier yet to say "Where's JoAnn?" and to speculate openly about her over coffee. Our conspiracy grew more out of proportion with each conversation. The subject almost became a form of office entertainment.

Meanwhile, JoAnn grew more and more distant from us.

One morning she came to work early. Her face was drawn and her eyes red. It was hard to make light of her trouble that day. She sat down very slowly.

"What is it?" I asked.

"It's personal," she said, and shook her head. That was all. She turned and began shuffling papers on her desk.

Kathy came and stood beside us. "Can I help?" she asked.

JoAnn shook her head. "Just find me that material for the annual report," she said. "I've got to get it done today."

Kathy moved away.

The three of us didn't talk about JoAnn after that. We watched her change from a bundle of energy to a tense shadow. She never regained her high spirits. An edge of bitterness grew in her tone of voice.

Finally, one day, without explanation, she resigned.

Her replacement was a thin little man without much sense of humor. I wished JoAnn were back.

When I think of her now, I'm reminded of the emptiness of our circle of gossip. JoAnn's pain and disintegration, when it came, hurt us all.

I wish now that I had done so many things differently. I

wish I had sat down by her desk one day and asked her how she was. She would not have told me, but she would have known I was there.

I wish that when she came in looking so distraught, I had asked again, and had tried to show her that I wanted to help. Even then, I can't be sure she'd have responded.

But she would not have gone away thinking that nobody cared, had she been willing to reach out for a friend. I think of JoAnn when I see other friends and acquaintances whose lives are bordering on some trouble. I pray for them, and I ask for some opportunity to help.

I believe now that the way to restoration lies not in gossip, but in true concern. I've vowed to learn that lesson and never repeat my mistake.

> And above all things have fervent charity among yourselves: for charity shall cover the multitude of sins.
>
> 1 Peter 4:8

# 16    Climbing Higher?🌿

"**D**o you think we'll ever be promoted?"

That was Kathy talking to me on our lunch break.

She'd been on the job a little longer than I. The thought of promotion had hardly crossed my mind; I was still trying to get a firm hold on the present situation.

Kathy, though, had seemed confident about her work ever since I came. I suppose she did feel ready for more.

"Things seem pretty well set the way they are," I observed. "Promoted to what?"

"I don't know," she said. "That's what worries me. Is this the kind of job that stays the same, month after month? I feel like I've already done everything so many times. I need a change."

"What would you like to do instead?" I asked. Kathy was one of our main client contacts. Most of the people who called up seemed to ask for her. I thought her easy handling of people and their request was impressive. If she were ever promoted, I wondered who else would do her job as well as she did it. "You're good at what you do," I said. "Don't you like it?"

"Sure," she said. "I'd just like to believe there's more."

A recent book crossed my mind as we talked. I'd been reading about a great shift in our American economy. At least one popular writer thinks there will be more and more

jobs like ours—service-type jobs, he calls them—and fewer upper-level jobs for all the new generations of business hopefuls who want to rise to the top.

The top is swollen, they say. Only a limited percentage of those who want to be there will ever make it. The high paying jobs will become scarce, but there will be a continuing demand for people who offer services or process information—insurance people and office record keepers, for instance. Customer oriented jobs like clerking and offering direct assistance of some kind will still be the mainstay of the American workplace. That means the middle-level, middle paying jobs—the jobs without much hope for promotion—will predominate.

We'll have to get used to being satisfied with the present, if these predictions hold up. That continual longing for something more, or better, or different will have to be altered into a more productive approach to our present lives. For many of us, that will take some re-evaluation.

Where Are You, God?

"Can you live without promotion?" I asked Kathy, just to see what she would say. "What would happen to you if things stayed the way they are?"

"It would be hard for me," she said, and I could see the honesty in her reply. "I'm young. I've got my whole future ahead of me. All through college I looked forward to getting somewhere with my life," she said.

I understood what she meant. I, too, had been raised on the "get ahead" philosophy. But I knew what the books today were warning: that we'll have to find our job satisfaction on a daily basis. We'll have to develop independent lives and take our fulfillment from outside activities or hobbies or friends.

I thought of two women I knew who worked at the large supermarket near me. One of them had worked there nearly seventeen years. I admired the way these two who were special to me greeted their customers as they came through the line, talking to them about their families and the week just past. They worked fast and efficiently, but they personalized their work through the people who came to them, week after week, standing in their line and no other. My weekend shopping was never complete without an encounter with Barbara or Virginia.

I knew, from things they said, that their jobs were not always easy or smooth, but I could see them making their lives work through the people who came to them. I thought of them when I became discouraged with my own work. I hoped I could be like them.

I doubted my examples would satisfy Kathy. The jobs they held were not encouraging when it came to promotion. But I told her my thoughts, anyway. I was heartened to think that wherever you are, you can make your own job satisfaction.

"I have to live as if today is all I might have," I said to her. "I'm not good enough at everything I have to do today. I know there's more I could find within my own job if I dug just a little deeper. I just can't worry yet about getting promoted. I'm not even sure it's a clear possibility, or something I should break my heart over."

"I can't understand you, Nancy," Kathy said. "That's not enough for me. I've got to believe there's more."

"I know what you're saying," I said. "I'm not being very helpful, am I? I guess I've been reading too many books lately. I'm sorry, Kathy."

She smiled at me and we stopped talking.

I actually suspected Kathy *would* be promoted. She was restless and energetic enough to make it happen. But it's not going to happen to everyone, in the measure we expect. And if it doesn't come to us, what then?

I believe we have all the resources of grace and thanksgiving we need, stored up from our daily walk with a God who can personalize each day. The light He gives to the moments that pass through our lives have often been "more than I could ever ask or think."

So I know He has even more light ahead.

... But be ye transformed by the renewing of your mind, that ye may prove what is that good, and acceptable, and perfect, will of God.

Romans 12:2

# 17

Sticking
Together🖋

"**H**arry's done it again."

I heard the whisper and stood up to see what Harry had done.

Hal and Kathy were leaning over an orange folder with a garish black banner strung across the top. Three dancing tigers jumped off the lower border. Tigers were the symbol of one of our clients.

Kathy shook her head.

"Maybe Johnson won't think it's so bad," Hal whispered to her. "Crumbs! It's awful, though."

We'd been sending out brochures like this to a local firm to design and print for us. We'd used Harry's services for over a year. Harry was the kind of person to bend over backwards and take extra time to make sure everything was just right—every word spelled exactly, and all that. You'd drive past his place at night and he'd always be there working. The light never went off at Harry's before 10:00 P.M.

Harry needed the work. He'd lost two other jobs because he was balding and a little slower than some of the younger men who had lots of talk and ideas. They'd always get promoted over him, he said. The last time he lost a job, his wife had just had her gall bladder out and spent days in the hospital with no insurance. Harry had gone into business for himself, to keep up a steady income. We couldn't stand to see things go bad for him again—all because of some dancing tigers.

That afternoon Harry came out of Mr. Johnson's office, looking glum.

Mr. Johnson came out after Harry had left. "That may be it for Harry," he said. "I hate to do it." He shook his head.

"Who's going to do all that detail work for us now?" Hal asked. "There isn't anyone in the office with the time to check on all the little things Harry checks for us."

Mr. Johnson looked at Hal a minute without comment. Then he stuck his hands deep in his pockets and looked like he was thinking.

"Can't we just show him *exactly* what we want?" I said. "Maybe even give him a design of how we want it to look?"

Mr. Johnson looked thoughtful.

"Sure, we could do that," Hal said.

"Maybe," Mr. Johnson said.

"Well, good," said Hal.

I held my breath. Mr. Johnson didn't like to be told what to do.

Hal picked up the orange brochure with the deep black lettering and the tigers. "Too late for this one," he said. "But wait till you see the next project. I'll have it all sketched out so there's no going wrong possible."

"Okay, I'll call Harry back," Mr. Johnson said. "Is that what you want?"

"Yes," Hal said with surprising firmness. "It's no good getting rid of people," Hal added. "Not unless they've done you wrong. Harry's got the best attitude of anyone here. We're rotten, next to Harry."

Mr. Johnson smiled.

"Guess we'd better stick with Harry. If we kept you two," he winked at Hal, "we can keep just about anybody."

I smiled at his comment. *It was true*, I thought. *Nobody's perfect. We accept that about each other most of the time.*

I followed Mr. Johnson to his office.

Where Are You, God?

"Harry really is okay," I said. "He works harder than almost any of us, and certainly longer. I like Hal's idea. If we can get a format that works, something that is all worked out instead of leaving it up to someone else, those problems just won't happen. I really think Harry is worth a lot."

"I'm considering all you've said today," Mr. Johnson said. "I've never really had to terminate anybody for hard work, come to think of it. Sloppy work, or rotten attitudes about the work or the office. Something like that, yes. But you're right. Harry needs our own teamwork. I'm willing to see if we can make things work better for him."

"Thanks," I said. "We'll all work on it, I know."

I felt relieved. After all, none of us is perfect, when you come right down to it. And it might be one of us on the line another time, needing the same kind of support.

I'm more and more convinced, through such experiences, that we need to find ways to help one another do our work better. If we can anticipate what someone else needs and fit our helping hands to that project, perhaps we can all come up with results that are better. After all, God takes us the way we are. He makes the best of us—sometimes better than we ever expected. If that's what God does, surely we can give it a try.

I felt very thankful for the heavenly precedent. Christ Himself had stood up for us—taken the ultimate risk "while we were yet sinners"—at a very high cost. Surely we could stand up for one another.

> . . . [Bear] with one another and [forgive] . . . one another, if anyone has a complaint against another; even as Christ forgave you, so you also must do.
>
> Colossians 3:13 NKJV

# 18

Allies🖋

---

The young woman across the table from me in the restaurant was out of a job. She'd been to our office to apply for one, to no avail. I knew her family from church and admired their generosity toward anyone who needed something. I knew, too, what it was like to feel there was no one who sensed your distress when you were out of work or feeling alone. When you're down and confused about the future, it helps to know there's someone who is pulling for you.

So I invited her to lunch.

"I can't seem to find anything," my friend was saying as I asked her how things were going. "Right now I'm waiting on tables, just as a stopgap. I'm not even using my college education."

She told me she was a psychology major. No one had ever taken the time to explain her career options to her. She was in the job market with no skills except "people skills."

"I need to get back to school," she said. "But I've got too many bills. I just can't do it right now."

I resisted the urge to say, "Oh, surely something will work out, in God's own time." I believed that, but it would sound superficial and would short-circuit our conversation.

"If you had a choice, what would you really like to do?" I asked her.

"I just want to help people," she said. "But that isn't getting me anywhere, I know. And it doesn't pay the rent."

"Help people how?" I asked. "You can help people wherever you are."

She nodded at me.

"What else can you do to go along with that?"

"Organize things, I suppose. . . and type . . . maybe even operate an office machine . . . I like those things."

"Job skills," I said. "Let me ask you something else. Have you tried a computer? That's where the future is, they say: word processing, or data entry, or something like that."

She shook her head.

"There's so much good software now," I added.

"Software?" She looked at me and frowned.

"It's a term," I said. "You'll learn all about it in a class or two. You should try a course in computers."

"Maybe," she said slowly. Then she added, "I really do know the Lord has an answer for me. It just hurts to wait for it, that's all. But I do believe He has something."

She said the hopeful words herself, surprising me. I didn't even need to preach to her.

"Good," I said. "Knowing *that* really does help. I know about the waiting. I've been where you are."

"How did you *stand* it?" she asked.

"I'd be so down I didn't want to see anybody," I said. "And then I'd read Philippians: 'I know how to be abased and I know how to abound—and I have learned the secret of facing plenty and hunger—and I can do all things through Christ who strengthens me.'" (Philippians 4:13 NKJV.)

"I'd read all that, and after a while, a peace would come to me, stopping my worry. Then I'd feel like making some phone calls, or going out for an interview, or doing something to help myself. I had to stop giving in to the panicky feeling."

*Is this making sense?* I wondered. *What works for me may not help someone else. But it's the same God in every situation, so maybe it does help.*

Her eyes brightened. "Philippians?" she said. "Let me write that down."

"I haven't been a whole lot of practical help," I said. "All I can say is, I understand where you are."

"That's a lot," she said. "I'll let you know if anything happens."

As we finished our lunch and stood outside the restaurant, I gave her my phone number. I wanted her to stay in touch. I wanted her to succeed.

I thought of the line from one of John Donne's devotions, "... every man is a piece of the Continent, a part of the main." It means we are all involved together in a shared human experience.

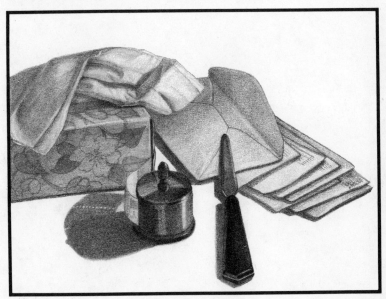

We need so much support from one another.

We must be allies in the name of Christ. What happens to one of us affects us all.

Bear ye one another's burdens, and so fulfill the law of Christ.

Galatians 6:2

# 19

Lag-Time
Theory

I tried hard to imagine a woman with five teenaged children, a nationally recognized medical career, and one hundred published articles to her credit.

I couldn't.

But here was the resumé, just arrived in the mail, saying Dr. Georgia Connor had done exactly that. She was coming to town to speak at the hospital dedication. It would be my job to take her to lunch and to write up her life story in a news release. This was one story I wanted to hear more about.

When I first saw her, I noticed how short she was—a dark-haired woman with piercing eyes and straight, tailored hair. Her speech at the morning dedication urged compassion as the key to the medical profession. She quoted from a favorite TV character in the television series "M*A*S*H" to prove her point: "Remember, the head bone is connected to the heart bone."

A famed cancer researcher, she seemed not one inch impressed by her own achievements. Becoming a humane professional above all else was her theme.

*Is that how it is when you're famous?* I wondered. *You don't have to impress anybody anymore?*

"How do you do it?" I asked her at lunch. "One hundred

articles, a recognized career in a major medical center, and five children?"

She smiled that quick, even flash, and her eyes crinkled. Her black hair glistened under the restaurant lamps. "It wasn't easy," she said. "No, it was hard work. If I meet a young person with ambition today, I feel compelled to tell her to stick it out. 'You'll get there,' I want to tell her. Good things take time."

"How much time?" I asked. "How long?"

I was not exactly young, and time was getting away from me.

Her eyes were sympathetic. "Always longer than you expect," she said.

"Tell me about the children," I said. "How did you handle all that? Five of them?"

"They mean a lot to me," she said. "To my husband, too. I spent every minute with them I could. I arranged my schedule to be sure we had time, especially on evenings and weekends."

"Oh," I said. I had heard all that before, and didn't know how she meant it.

"I refused to believe the advice that children come second," she said. "I can't accept that."

Here was the key I was searching for.

"Your husband helped you, then?"

"Yes. Of course. But mostly he encouraged me not to give up. He could see how much I wanted to do medicine. He had the bigger medical jobs at first, and I had the little ones. I think that's how it had to work for a while, or at least that's how it seems to work for many of us who have families."

"He starts out ahead of you professionally, while you pedal along behind?"

"Yes. Sort of. It couldn't be helped. I had to remember that. I was tempted to blame him, because he was so far ahead of me for a while. But he was the one who encouraged me to keep on."

"And then?"

"Things started happening. The kids were older, for one thing. I was invited to take this bigger job, and I was ready for it. After that everything started to happen for me."

"Like . . . ?"

"Like, I wasn't discouraged anymore. I began catching up. I could feel myself coming closer to my ideas of feeling challenged and fulfilled."

"How long ago?" I asked. "Has it been a long time now?"

"I'm fifty-five," she said. "It was about ten years ago . . . twelve, maybe."

"Only ten years ago? That was a long wait," I said.

"Maybe. It doesn't seem so anymore," she said. Her voice trailed off for a minute. "Now, what about you?" she asked. Her eyes were suddenly kind. "Tell me about you."

I shrugged my shoulders. "Not much to tell," I said. "I have ideas. They're still out there, somewhere."

"They'll come closer," she said. "I have a theory. I call it the lag-time theory. I think women take longer to reach their peak than men. I'm almost sure of it."

"Really?" She was a specialist in psychiatry and cancer, and I gathered she had studied the subject of human behavior a little.

"If you know that theory, it makes you more patient," she said. "It gives the waiting more meaning." She looked at me and smiled. "What else can I tell you?" she asked. "Have you got enough information for your story?"

"You've told me a lot," I said. I looked at my notes. I had six pages full of details about her family, her restored New England home, her children's career plans, her husband. "You're very generous," I said.

And then we stood up to leave.

It was one of those moments when you want to say something very flowery. But there are no words.

I thanked God as we stood there for lives that reach outward toward other people and keep ambition in its place;

for people who see beyond themselves, to those who need them.

I determined that whatever happened to me, I would never forget her lesson.

Beloved, let us love one another: for love is of God . . . .
1 John 4:7

# 20

## In Search of Models🌿

"**H**ave you noticed," Kathy whispered, "that we're almost the only women at this meeting?"

I hadn't. The room was filled with managers in search of better customer techniques. Kathy and I were there at the request of Mr. Johnson, who was too busy to attend this one-day seminar and thought one of us should go in his place. We both expressed an interest, so he sent us both.

"We've got to do something," Kathy said. "And soon. Things have got to change."

It crossed my mind that maybe Mr. Johnson was already doing something. At least, he had sent us here today.

As I looked around, I wondered, too, why there weren't more of us. There are times when you feel you're on the way across a long bridge, a part of a long, slow march of history, and you just have to accept that. Things will change, though never fast enough for our human timetable. The thought comforted me.

What I feared most, as I thought of it, was the reaction of some women who suddenly achieve titles and status. Sometimes they seemed unprepared for it, as if the new and stirring experience had jarred their thinking.

I had stood in the public library just last week, talking to an older employee about her husband's recent heart attack.

As we talked, a younger woman I knew came and stood between us.

"I need to give you some material for next week's public-service announcement," she interrupted, without waiting her turn. She began to talk to me as if she had the prior right to my attention.

My older friend left us while this young woman, newly promoted, conducted her business with me. The incident, with her assumption of authority, is a painful memory. I hoped that if I ever had the opportunity to move upward, I would not overlook my colleagues or become callous toward them.

"We don't have many good models yet," I said aloud to Kathy. "That's the hard part."

"Yes," she said. "We don't even know what kind of rules to play by, or how so many things should work. We've never even been groomed for leadership—most of us."

She was right. I could hardly think of a single woman in a leadership role that I wanted to be like. Or could I?

There was Dr. Georgia Connor, who had achieved national scientific fame but still cared more about people than about almost anything else. There was my friend Fran, the first female personnel director at her firm, as warmhearted toward God and man as a person could be. And if I thought harder, there were a few others, too. But in our own building, within our own company, the examples of real leadership among women were hard to find.

"We'll have to find our own way, Kathy," I said. "I'll help you, if you'll help me."

"Right," she said. "Let's hang in there for each other."

I nodded, thoughtfully.

The meeting was coming to order, so we turned to the front of the room, but my mind drifted away once more. I thought of the two women recorded in Scripture who stayed very close to Jesus—Mary and Martha. Martha was "cumbered" with much serving, and distressed about her work, we're told. Mary chose to sit a long time at the feet of Jesus and hear His words, while Martha hustled and fretted about. I knew that didn't mean we should avoid working mightily, for Martha worked hard. But I'm sure Jesus intended that, like Mary, we keep our eyes beyond ourselves and our own responsibilities—that we always keep the heavenly perspective. Life is first of all love of God Himself and of our neighbors. Our own status among others shrinks very small next to that.

But seek ye first the kingdom of God, and his righteousness . . . .

Matthew 6:33

# 21

## The Greatest of These . . . 🖋

Sometimes you meet people who bring you up short about your own attitudes toward life and work.

I first met Rowena when I moved to Texas, four years ago. I only saw her once a week or less, when I stood in her line at the checkout counter at K-Mart. But her bright spirit was always contagious, and she lifted my spirits as I left the store.

After a few weeks, I began to feel cheated if Rowena happened to be out or away for the day. She was the most consistently cheerful person I had ever met.

"How's everyone today?" she'd ask, calling out to us as we came through the door. She could make us feel as if we were the only ones in the store. She seemed glad to see us, week after week, in more than a superficial way.

It was my husband who noticed her first and began our regular encounters with her during our Saturday shopping outings. He picked her out because he's an avid cashier watcher and she never rang up anything incorrectly.

"Let's try her line," he said to me one day. "I think she really knows what she's doing." And she did. My husband seemed satisfied that she rang up things right, and he began to talk with her.

I think she sensed his admiration. She talked warmly to us as she rang things up, still maintaining her accuracy. She had raised six children, she said, seen two of them through college, and then enjoyed their pursuit of the best of life's goals. She talked with enthusiasm about their work, their hopes of promotion, their interest in working with people. She asked us about our own teenagers, too, and listened to us with interest.

What were the sources of her good nature and her strength from week to week? I wondered as I watched her. Sometimes, as we chatted, I wondered if she, too, had her hard days. I watched her face sometimes, wondering. But if there was anything—and I later learned she'd had more than her share of life's pain—she never let on as she waited on us with enthusiasm. Her warmth of interest toward us was always reflected in her face as she put her own problems aside.

She became a kind of model to me in several ways, after a while. Day after day, for more than ten years, she had stood in this store, checking out merchandise fast and accurately and talking warmheartedly to people. I learned there were dozens of other people like us who would only stand in her line, even if it was long.

I'm ashamed when I think how easily my work and my approach to others is affected by the ups and downs of my daily life. Rowena flashes to my mind on those days—always the same and glad to see us. As I encountered her week after week, I grew in my desire to focus outward on others more than on myself. I've made that desire a matter of prayer, and so I've found that the outward focus does not come easily to most of us.

*Lord*, I thought, *show me how she does it*. I wasn't even sure she could tell me how, if I asked her. She would probably be surprised at the question. For her, being this way with people was a lifetime habit and a God-given gift. I was making a late beginning and would probably never catch up with her. But as I prayed, I realized that with God all things are possible.

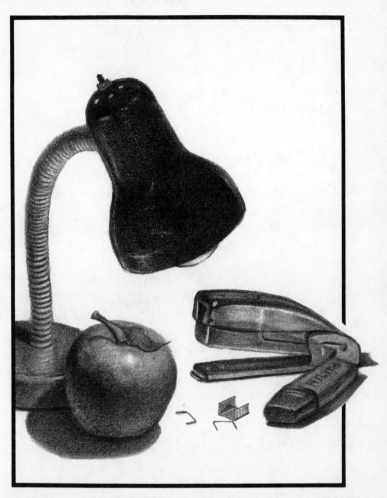

I saw that if I am willing to seek those gifts that Christ offers us in Scripture, God can use my desire for an outward focus of love and gradually transform my daily life. Good things come slowly. But at least I know for certain that God is the giver of every good gift—warmth and love included.

Beloved, let us love one another: for love is of God . . . .

1 John 4:7

# 22

## Promotion, Money, and a More Excellent Way🍃

Why is there always less money in the checking account than we expected? If we could earn just a little more, we would be so much better off, we think.

Rarely does money work that way. No matter how much it increases from year to year, we've spent it before we even have it, and there is never any left over. We've struggled, and fretted, and finally received an increase, only to be in the same bind all over again.

I was paying bills one Saturday morning, just after an ample increase marking my second year with this job, when I realized there would never be enough money. At first I'd been very careful with it, but gradually I had added to my regular monthly expenses, and the children as they grew older had added even more. Now I had to hold the line on the fifteenth of the month and just grit my teeth until the next pay, two weeks later. My stomach began to feel very tight when it came time to pay the bills again.

It struck me one day that I was not alone in my dilemma. I don't know why it was such a surprise to think that God knew all about it, too. In fact, it was really *His* money that I was spending, not mine at all.

That thought didn't change the pile of bills I had to pay, but the realization did seem to change something, all the same.

In my mind I saw again the multitudes gathered in the countryside, waiting expectantly for Jesus to feed them. And I saw the five loaves and two small fishes He had broken up into fragments so that it could stretch to fill the demand. *Five loaves and two fishes*, I thought. *Not nearly enough, and yet somehow plenty.*

This money in my checkbook seemed suddenly like the five loaves and the two fishes. If it was God's money, and not mine, then He could break it into whatever fragments would satisfy the needs lying all around me on the bills that had come in.

As I prayed and tried to envision my money that way, I gradually saw my bills whittle down over the weeks. I discovered that my worst fears never came to be. I never really sank under my financial obligations.

Somehow, viewing my finances as the Lord's and not mine did something else as well. I began to find ways to give to others out of God's provision for me. I had the same amount of money as before, but I never ran out.

What was even better, some unlooked for friendships developed as a result of my responding to the needs of other people. I found myself looking more to the concerns of my friends and less to my own personal and financial advancement.

I realized how much my thinking had changed when Kathy came up to my desk and said, "Do you realize how underpaid we are? I've been checking around, and we're at the bottom end of the national scale. What do you think we ought to do?"

Her face was serious and strained.

"Do?" I said. I felt no impulse to respond. Somehow the battle for my own advancement seemed less interesting than ever before. "I don't know," I said.

Kathy looked at me, disappointed.

It wasn't that I had no energy for a crusade. It was just

that this crusade didn't stir me. "Be content with what you have," I remembered.

I tried to explain. But I realized as I talked that every person has to see it for herself, as if for the first time. You can't see it for her. "I'm sorry," I said. "I do understand how you feel. I'm just not where you are, right now. My life is making sense without that. But I'll help you, if you want me to."

She shrugged her shoulders. "I'll get back to you," she said. "Thanks."

Three days later, Mr. Johnson called me into his office unexpectedly and shut the door. "We've decided to give you a title change," he said, "and a small increase in salary next month. What do you say to that?"

I could find no response. The timing, now that I had decided to set aside my desire to push for advancement, caught me off guard. I sat very still for a minute.

"Thank you, Mr. Johnson," I finally said. "I'm not sure I can explain to you how grateful I am. I wish that I could. You've made my day, in more ways than you know."

He nodded and smiled.

*God is faithful*, I thought. *Five loaves and two fishes—and twelve baskets left over.*

Seek ye first the kingdom of God, and his righteousness; and all these things shall be added unto you.

Matthew 6:33

# 23 A Sense of Perspective🌿

Pressure, materialism, and internal politics: sometimes these crosscurrents seem to be the daily reality. I try to ignore them as best I can on the days they bother me. They aren't the things that matter in God's scheme. There's another invisible world that money cannot buy.

Sometimes we encounter that message in unexpected places, as we go about our daily work.

I was making a routine visit to a client one day, to drop off some material we'd written for him and to pick up his photograph. He was a member of the city council, representing the Hispanic vote in the local population. He was newly elected, and people said he was doing a good job.

"How are things?" I said casually, as he greeted me. "I read good things in the newspaper about you."

His law degree and two college diplomas hung on the wall above his swivel chair. He spoke three languages fluently. As he leaned toward me, his chair squeaked. "Things are fine," he said. "How about with you?"

He looked interested. I shrugged off the question. "Not as fine as with you," I said.

"I'll tell you one thing," he said, perhaps sensing that I held some illusions about his success. "It's hard work here. So many people to please. I have to remind myself why I'm here, some days."

"Oh?" I said.

"I mean, it was a long way from where I started to this office," he said. "I don't ever want to forget. I don't want to take anything for granted."

I blinked at him. He was obviously at the top of almost everything right now. Was he still struggling, too?

"When I was twenty, I didn't even speak English," he said. "Can you believe that?"

I really couldn't. He was very articulate.

"I was born in another country," he said. "I never even heard English, and I learned to read and write it on my own. When I went to college, I couldn't even understand the lectures."

I nodded. "How did you come all this way?" I said.

"I came up to Texas to preach to my people," he said. "But I realized right away I needed an education. I didn't have any money, so I was stopped in my plans. Then a college offered to help me and I went all the way through. I was up in my twenties when I graduated."

He looked at me, to see if I wanted him to keep on. Something in my face must have answered his question.

"It was the Lord's help to me," he said. "I can't explain it otherwise. When I meet people today who have problems, I like to tell them about my long struggle. I didn't have anything at all, and I got an education anyhow. With the Lord, anybody can do anything.

"We get to thinking everybody's always had everything," he said. "Life isn't like that for most people."

I had no reply for him. This man had made it all the way against odds I would never know anything about.

*Power, money, success—what are they?* I thought. They weren't the reasons he was sitting here today.

I sat quietly a minute, nodding at him, and he smiled and nodded at me. Then his phone rang. Quickly, I thanked him. I left him talking on the phone and he nodded good-bye to me.

I pondered his story all the way back to the office.

When I walked to my desk, Hal looked angry about something. My train of thought snapped back to our pressured world.

"What's wrong here?" I asked.

"Politics," Hal mumbled. "Everybody's pushing everybody else around as if there's no tomorrow. I can't stand it!"

He was drawing little black circles with his ballpoint pen. I watched, thinking how far from this world I had been just a few minutes ago. I sat down and repeated my experience at City Hall.

Hal listened a long time, and laid his pen down. "Thanks for telling me," he said quietly. "I needed that today."

"Thanks for listening," I said. "I had to tell somebody."

Little did either of us know how very soon we would need to remember the lesson. We were about to enter a time when office politics seemed more important than anything else in the world.

Do not be deceived, my beloved brethren. Every good . . . and . . . perfect gift is from above, and comes down from the Father of lights, with whom there is no variation or shadow of turning.

James 1:16, 17 NKJV

# 24

Power
Shifts🖋

"**M**r. Johnson has an announcement," Kathy said, coming to the side of my desk. "He said to meet in his office at ten-thirty." She looked very expectant. "Mr. Rogers is coming in, too," she said.

Mr. Rogers was one of the owners of the company. We rarely saw him.

At ten-thirty, Hal and Kathy and I, and the others on the staff, crowded into Mr. Johnson's square office, some of us standing for lack of seats. Mr. Johnson stood, too, and Mr. Rogers sat at the desk with a piece of paper in his hand. When everyone was there, he began to read from it.

"With great appreciation for the loyalty of Mr. Carl Johnson's many years of service," he read, "I regretfully accept his resignation. Mr. Johnson has informed me that he will be accepting a position with Texas Graphics Incorporated."

He cleared his throat and looked at us, one by one. "During this interim," he continued, "I have asked Miss Kathy Morgan to serve as temporary director of operations until further notice." He laid the paper down on the desk and looked at us. "Any questions?" he asked.

It was one of those times when nobody knew quite how to react, whether to seem depressed or excited at a prospect of change. We had no questions.

We let Mr. Rogers stand up and leave the room in silence.

"Well, that's it," Mr. Johnson said to us in a monotone after Mr. Rogers was gone.

We nodded, looking at him.

"Wish you the best," Hal said. "Really."

Mr. Johnson nodded. "Thank you, Hal."

"Yes," I said. "I'm sure you'll like it where you're going." Then I let my guard down a little and added, "What will happen here, Mr. Johnson?"

"You'll be fine. Kathy will take good care of things." Mr. Johnson said it quickly, trying to sound positive.

I knew he was trying to make it easier for Kathy to carry on. It would be the first time the three of us who had carried a lot of the office workload would be consciously divided by rank. Hal and I were both older than Kathy; how would she handle her promotion over us?

Kathy was thin lipped and silent. She looked anxiously at us now. I could see she was worried. She wondered how we would accept her new status. It wouldn't do her any good at all to have the new rank, if we wouldn't play the game.

A lot would depend, at first, on how Kathy handled things. When you suddenly find yourself in charge, you have to win the team over to your side.

Kathy's first approach, as I remember it, was to send us lots of memos filled with her new ideas and agenda for the week. Hal would read them and stuff them back into his mailbox. I would file them away. Kathy would stay in her office and wait to see what we would do. Kathy's memos were far too long and filled with information about meetings she was attending and about her great new plans for the office.

The plans sounded fine, but they didn't have any teeth in them. Everything depended on Hal and me and the others picking up the ideas and running with them. We didn't feel much like implementing any of Kathy's ideas, since in the past we'd been encouraged to come up with our own.

Kathy sat in her office and waited for our response. She busied herself with the usual details of her editing job and kept up contacts with her specific clients.

I know now what I did not know then: Kathy suddenly found herself in one of the most difficult situations in the working world. Being promoted within the same office means you have to completely rethink all your relationships and then work hard at turning them around to fit the new pattern. It's something that can't be done by memo but only by personal interaction.

It was hard for her and for us, because we were used to the old patterns. It's almost better to be promoted to a fresh new situation than to have to transform an old one.

As I watched Kathy struggle, I began to feel the importance of helping her make her new leadership work. We were pulling against her, making her prove herself. The more we held back, the longer it would take.

"Lord, You know all about this," I prayed. "Help her.

Help all of us. We'll need to make this work. We have to get back to normal."

I knew God was not a keeper of disorder. Believing that, I knew we must work very hard for peace and harmony. If we did whatever we could to make things work better, God would take it from there. I decided not to join in with the others when they were tempted to complain about Kathy. That was the least I could do. If we were patient, Kathy would figure things out for herself, and things would start working better again.

> If it is possible, as much as depends on you, live peaceably with all men.
>
> Romans 12:18 NKJV

# 25 New Management Styles🖋

One thing about Mr. Johnson: He had enough power to get what he wanted. When he said, "jump," people tended to do just that.

With Kathy in charge, people tended to go on about their business without consulting her. I kept watching to see what she would do. She would have to establish her own management style.

At ten o'clock every day Hal and some of the others started slipping away for a coffee break. They gathered across the street at Lyon's Cafeteria and often came back disgruntled a few minutes later. Hal seemed almost snappish a couple of times.

Mr. Johnson's personal electricity must have made Kathy's no-nonsense work charts seem inhumane by contrast. The whispered word around the office was that Kathy was a "tyrant" and that she had no "real" leadership ability—whatever the "real" thing was.

As the unspoken seesaw of opinion grew, I felt caught in the middle. If I joined in with the others, I'd appear to be siding against Kathy, which I determined not to do. If I pulled away from the talk, I'd appear to have staked everything on Kathy's success. That would alienate me from everyone—perhaps permanently.

"Kathy's got some pretty sterile ideas," Hal muttered one day. "There's just no life in this place anymore."

*What should I say now?* Hal was waiting for my reaction. "You're a hard man to please," I quipped lightly. "Besides, you've still got plenty of life in you, Hal!"

The moment passed safely. A "soft answer turneth away wrath," I recalled. A soft answer must be anything that doesn't fan the flames and make them leap higher. I'd learned months earlier from the incident with JoAnn that negative feelings are intensified by voicing them to others. I still marvel sometimes at the power of words to bring into being "things that are not."

The dissension over Kathy remained just an undertone. It never really broke out of bounds to challenge her head-on. All it did was slow up our operation and keep it for many weeks at an unproductively slower pace. I'm not sure Kathy even realized it.

I wondered if our stalemated office situation was the kind of thing that frustrated God. It was hard to know how to pray, except for harmony. I'd always thought that God's chief concern was His heavenly kingdom. *How does an office busy with mundane matters fit into His priorities?* I wondered.

If I were God, though, I'd wipe everything clean here and start over from scratch. I couldn't see any other way to make things work. But if God did that, I'd be out of a job. So would Hal and Kathy and everyone else in the office.

I was thankful that God is more merciful than I. His tolerance and refusal to start over every time something goes wrong reminded me to be more patient. God seems to put up with a lot of imperfection, for reasons we know little about.

Perhaps He knows that our temporary muddling is preparing us for something just beyond what we can see. Scripture promises that nothing is wasted in a life where God is close at hand.

I wonder if at the last trumpet many of us will still be sitting at our desks puzzling over these things. Maybe we'll be taken completely by surprise by something far more wonderful than anything we know how to imagine.

At any rate, suddenly one day Kathy came to life. She called a meeting in her little office. We had to spill over into the big office outside, because hers was too small.

"I've been taking my time," she said, "doing my homework on what directions we should take. I've decided I need your views on how these ideas fit our work right now."

She began to outline her plan. When she finished, she turned to us for comment. At first everyone was silent, eyeing her to see if she could pull off her first attempt to change her style and to communicate with us.

Suddenly Hal seemed to take up her cause. "All right, everybody—for the suitcase and the trip to Paris. Whoever speaks up first is the sweepstakes winner!"

His words broke the ice, and the laughter started. Kathy threw back her head and laughed, too—a good sign. Suddenly Joseph, who worked in the area next to ours, described his recent assignments and offered an observation about Kathy's plan.

"The winner!" Hal said.

And then Hal began to talk, too. Before long, everybody had taken a turn, and Kathy was working out a flowchart on a green chalkboard. Within an hour she had the whole office on a schedule.

I have to admit, it was the best planning session our office had ever seen. Mr. Johnson drove us by the force of his personality, but Kathy would steer a course by her well-organized wits.

I may have resisted her leadership, but I could see she had worked out exactly what we needed. Her logic and planning might pay off.

I determined to make things easier for her. It was the least

I could do, and some Scripture I had been reading was urging me to build bridges with Kathy.

I think she sensed my support, because she began to seek my help and she asked for assistance with some of her old duties—things she'd once hoarded as too precious to be shared with anyone. That has to be one of the marks of the successful transition to a new position: the willingness to let someone else do the jobs you once prized as your own. They may be tasks you once staked your reputation on.

I was surprised Kathy could give some of those things up. Some of the jobs she asked me to do were ones no one had ever known about before: filing regular reports to top management and maintaining very close contact with the best clients. Now I found myself calling on some of these people and familiarizing myself with their old accounts.

Hal seemed to have cheered up, too. He was banging out work on his old typewriter with renewed zest, as if he enjoyed having a clear sense of what we were all about.

At least for the time being, Kathy had made a good start. She wasn't going to be a Mr. Johnson, but she was going to use her own special abilities very effectively.

I believed that God Himself would help me find my way with this new plan. If He would help me, surely He would help Kathy and the others, I believed. And as time went on, we began to reach out toward one another.

No, it wasn't perfect, just as it hadn't been perfect under Mr. Johnson. But I'm convinced that by a prayerful attitude we can live within our own circumstances and see them transformed by a power beyond our own.

As we accept new ways of doing things, we find new ways of fitting our own skills into the total structure. New management means an opportunity for review of what we're all about. Sometimes we need that, just to learn flexibility. God doesn't make perfect people or perfect situations in this present time frame. He lets us make our own mistakes and then learn to deal with them. I'm thankful for forgiveness, and mercy, and renewed chances to do better next time. That must be part of what our pilgrimage on this earth is all about.

Therefore let us not judge one another anymore, but rather resolve this, not to put a stumbling block or a cause to fall in our brother's way.

Romans 14:13 NKJV

Therefore receive one another, just as Christ also received us, to the glory of God.

Romans 15:7 NKJV

# 26

# Have No
# Idols🌿

It's true that new challenges on the job do a lot to give you a lift. But there's a catch to it all: the danger of turning work into an idol when things suddenly go well. Work is an idol not worth having.

I had been charged with a new responsibility: to write a marketing plan that would cover the services offered by every department in our company. I had never been asked to be so involved before. The assignment was a compliment, and I threw myself into the project.

I never worked so hard. I telephoned everyone whose input and information I needed. I drew up tables and charts and graphs. Finally I put together a rough, handwritten version of a long report.

I turned on my word processor, drew up my chair, and began to compose the final version of the report. I hardly glanced up for three hours. In the distance, I heard telephones ring and other people answering them. I heard lights clicking off, and soon I was the only person left—working late, as the world went about its evening business.

I didn't finish until almost seven o'clock. At home, they would have eaten, without me, the casserole I had prepared early that morning. I thought of them, thanked them. And I sat back in my chair at last . . . done.

I smiled at the work before me on the computer screen,

checked it for errors, and then turned on the printer to print it out. Fifteen crisp pages. Three more to come tomorrow, when I added the charts and graphs. The pages felt good in my fingers. I carefully set the report in the middle of the desk and laid a heavy brass paperweight over it. I stared at it and sat very still. Finally I stood up, snapped out the light, and looked back from the doorway. I did not feel tired at all. The work had energized me. I had poured my life into that report, and I felt good.

I walked outside slowly and found my car, sinking into the seat and dropping my keys into my lap. Suddenly I was very tired, after all. But I felt I had given my all, and I liked that feeling.

That night, as I slept fitfully and waited eagerly for the morning, I passed the time going over the pages again in my mind. I felt pleased every time I thought of the report. It seemed thorough and complete.

The next morning I felt very tired. At breakfast, I hardly spoke to anyone. The report swirled through my mind.

When we all finally left the house to go in our many workaday directions—some to school and some to places of employment—I sank into the car again and headed straight back to the office as if I had never left.

Driving along, I suddenly realized that I had not thought of anything but my report for hours, maybe even two days.

I looked out the car window. Outside, the sun was shining. The sky was a clear blue. It reminded me of my daughter, who had left the house wearing her favorite blue dress. I remembered how the blue set off her clear blue eyes and her white-blonde hair.

At lunch today, I would be meeting a friend I hadn't seen for several days. In the evening, my husband and I were going to a concert. I thought of all those good things and put the report out of my mind.

*What really matters most?* I asked myself. *That report sitting*

*on my desk waiting for me? Or the people around me and the beauti-
ful world outside, surrounding me with its natural bounty?*

I saw I had lost my perspective. I had been walking with
blinders on through this beautiful world of God's making.
How much had I missed, lost in the world of my own
smaller achievement?

I began to breathe deeply.

The work mattered, of course. I enjoyed the good feeling
that I had done my best.

But I knew I must beware of using my work to shut out
everything else around me. No paper, or any other product
or achievement on earth, was worth such a heavy price.

I remembered the words of John, when he wrote to the
early Christians, "Little children, keep yourselves from
idols" (1 John 5:21). Today I understood what those words
meant. I had almost created an idol. How easy it had been! I
had enjoyed it.

Keep your perspective, God was saying to me.

I was thankful once again for the wisdom of God's whole-
ness.

> And we know that the Son of God has come and has given
> us an understanding, that we may know Him who is true . . .
> Little children, keep yourselves from idols.
>
> 1 John 5:20, 21 NKJV

# 27 Tranquillity— or Boredom? 🍃

$S$ometimes a year can pass, or two, and everything seems to be going fine. Work evens out, everyone gets used to one another, and the office runs with hardly a hitch.

There's just one trouble: Too much tranquility can become boring. I had longed, during so many ups and downs, for peaceful times. Now that I finally had peace, I discovered boredom.

If I wasn't careful now, I would die on the job. After so many months of trying to find my way and become adjusted to the constant changes in people, routines, assignments, I felt I had everything under control. The office was pleasant and the work secure.

I had to ask myself, *What next?*

My concern seemed almost ironic. I had gotten the stability I had prayed for so long and so desperately. "Thank You, Lord, for peace," I had prayed. I still wanted to mean that prayer, but after so many weeks of peace, I began to worry. *What would become of me now?* I seemed to be standing still.

The work—more and more of the same—began to lose its flavor. I found myself putting it off, staring at it piled up before me. At last, I would plunge into the work, hurry through it, and hope to have enough time left over at the

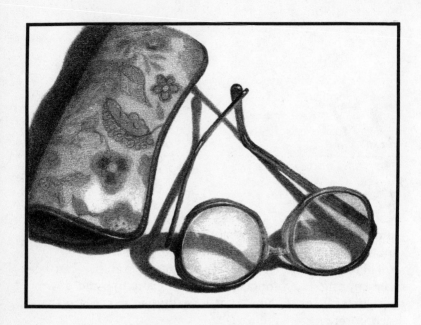

end of the day to daydream a little and generate some interesting thoughts of my own.

Getting the work done so I could have a few work-free moments became about the only motivation I could find. I seemed to have nothing to feel excited about anymore.

I tried to decide what to do. I watched Hal, always whistling at his desk, sipping coffee, casually making his way through the piles of work—a picture of contentment.

And Kathy, the door to her office usually open, talking incessantly on the telephone to customers, getting all the motivation she needed from the requests that came in. She never seemed to tire of her work.

So what was wrong with me? Why was tranquillity such a problem only to me?

I knew it was because I had always wanted a sense of moving forward, a sense of direction and purpose, a sense that I was part of some great plan that God was unfolding in

Where Are You, God?

my life. Sitting or standing still had never seemed part of that desire to move forward with God.

Was that desire too much to ask of God? It seemed to be more than others asked for from their jobs. And yet, I realized, we were all different. For me, even the simplest thing must have meaning. I had learned to accept that fact about myself and not to fault others if they found some different way toward satisfaction.

I shut my eyes a minute and pictured my work, pictured everything about my days here. I sensed that whatever God had for me must be beyond the immediate world of my desk. I knew I could only become happy from within and that I must do my work because of that inner happiness.

Job satisfaction cannot come from the job, but only from within. I had no control over the external flow of the ups, downs, and dull moments in the world outside me. I could only be responsible for what was on the inside.

"There is great peace in godliness with contentment" (*see* 1 Timothy 6:6), I remembered reading in the Bible. And in another place I recalled the words, "Let this mind be in you, which was also in Christ Jesus" (Philippians 2:5).

What mind was that? It seemed to be a mind that took on the form of a servant. Somehow, in the attitude of Christ, even the quietest day should have its own inner certitude.

I decided to seek in fuller measure that quality of life that depended on no circumstances. God had brought me to utter boredom to say to me, "Be still. Look beyond your work. For I have something better than any temporary change of activity. I have the peace that passes all your understanding, and the joy that no man (or moment) taketh from you."

In my tranquillity, or boredom, I must learn to direct my hunger and thirst in other directions: toward God, ever present, at my elbow, at my desk, suddenly emerging in conversations with others, popping out unexpectedly in blessings I must be watching for. Small things from the hand of God could make every day its own occasion for praise.

But I needed to be looking for them. Such expectancy could only come from a change of focus. In all circumstances, I must practice the understanding that God is ever with me.

The eyes of your understanding being enlightened; that ye may know what is the hope of his calling . . . .
                                                      Ephesians 1:18

# 28

Setbacks🌿

---

O ne day everything is fine, quiet, a matter of routine. The next day, without warning, the sky falls.

It can be a little piece of the sky, or the whole thing. Whatever it is, it feels devastating and final when it happens.

"You're being transferred."

That news greeted me early one morning when I had just begun to get a grasp of several new responsibilities. I was feeling good about my work. I had ahold of things, and I understood the inner working of the office procedures.

Why change now? The news did not make sense.

"It's for your own good," I was told. "And for the good of everyone in the office. We are redistributing job assignments. We think this new arrangement will work better. You'll be moving upstairs."

I looked out my window. I had the perfect view, out across a fountain and a long row of trees. In my window hung a basket of orange and red silk nasturtiums that danced in the bright light. From my desk I could look directly out the window. Trees and sunshine always made me work better.

Upstairs, there were no windows. I would be in the middle of a large area with several others, separated only by the arrangement of office furniture.

Setbacks                                                                127

I would have to hang some pictures somewhere, to remind me of the trees.

I realized that I feared change. I could think only of the disadvantages and of all that would be lost. Oh, the loss. We let go of things with such heavy hearts.

But why this change? Why now?

The truth was, there would be more responsibility with my new job after a while, I was told. And more "creative input." I should be "glad of the opportunity," I was advised.

So why wasn't I?

Perhaps because I, and so many others who were affected, had not been consulted. We'd had no idea the change was coming. Like so many things in the working world, sudden alterations in plans seem to come without warning to those who do not make the plans.

All I could feel was shock. And then anger. And then helplessness. *It isn't fair*, I thought. It's never fair.

I didn't like the feelings that swirled over me, but I did not try to push them back. I had learned the hard way that suppressing feelings only bottles them up for another less appropriate time. It was appropriate to feel all these things now; I must let the feelings come.

I turned my back so nobody could see me, and I let the tears come. At noon, I went out for a long walk. When I finally grew tired, I found a place where I could sit down. The wind blew across my face, and in the distance a bird cried with me. The sun was fading and the clouds rolled in.

"Lord, I'm hurting," I prayed. "I know, as I did not know once, that You care. Thank You for tears. For pain. For this honesty to say how I feel."

I did not think about tomorrow or the positive thoughts I would experience later. I only thought of what was really there today—of my pain and surprise and shock—of my fear that somehow in the impersonality of corporate planning I had been abandoned. I cried again, real tears. And I was thankful for a God who could say to me, "I care how

Where Are You, God?

you feel," and did not require shallow optimism of me when my heart was overcome with pain.

I felt the calm of understanding. I thought of the everlasting arms of the Old Testament and of a heavenly empathy with my condition that had sent God all the way to a cross to die for what I could not change. I was thankful for a God who had paid every price of pain and suffering so that I could cry today about my own real pain. I thanked God that my tears mattered.

I will not leave you comfortless: I will come to you.

John 14:18

# 29 Change: What Does It Mean? 🌿

The office was very quiet all afternoon. Everyone was working, telephones were ringing, people came and went with their various requests. Nobody wanted to talk. Not yet. Not only was I being transferred, but so were several others. We were involved in a complete office shake-up that would affect everyone before it was over.

I had been thinking all day how I would be affected and how my life would change because of it. But everyone was involved. Even the slightest change involves everyone.

And this was not a slight change. When it was over, we would all be in a different relation to one another than we had ever seen before. Some of us would be removed to new locations. Nothing would ever be the same.

It was too soon to talk. Each of us was imagining how it would be. We had our initial flurry of conversation about it, exchanged all the information we had heard, and now we had turned silent. Each of us was looking inward, to see how he would be affected. Later we would be talking again, but not today.

Kathy's office door was closed. She was lucky enough to have an office with a door, so she could close herself off from us. She would be going, too—to a better situation. But it meant she would be leaving the city to work for a branch office. She wouldn't even be a part of our operation anymore.

I thought she would miss us. But I thought she was glad to be going, too, to be putting our problems behind her, if only to take up new ones. I thought of the people I would be working with more closely, and of the ones I would see even less.

Every change is a kind of death, I decided: a loss, an occasion for grief before beginning over again. And we have to walk the entire cycle of disbelief, acceptance, regret, and acknowledgement of our pain, before we can go on.

The silence in our office said we were doing some of that today.

I answered a phone call, heavyhearted. "May I help you?" I said, hoping the request would be a small one.

"I need a complete revision of last year's annual report brochure," the voice said. "Can you update the figures and rewrite the introduction—brighten it up a bit? We want an upbeat sound to it this year."

The annual report—I'd forgotten it. This was a project that took concentration, and I'd never liked doing it. Right now I didn't feel like doing it at all. "I'll pull it out of the file," I said.

"We need the first draft next Friday," the voice said.

"Friday?" My voice was slow, strained.

"Well, Tuesday of the next week will be all right, then. Will Tuesday be better?"

"I think Tuesday will work," I said.

"Good. Tuesday, then."

I hung up the phone and laid the report slowly on the top of my pile of things to do. I hoped I'd find the enthusiasm for it soon. Today was not a day for pushing ahead.

When you're in transition, you lose the flow of your work for a while. The mind needs time to turn itself. It's a natural part of the process of change. I hoped the people who were drawing up new plans for the office understood that. We would try very hard not to let the work slip, but our minds were turning in other directions, and it was hard to bring them back. Keeping on in the midst of change is the hardest thing of all.

I began to pray, because I knew that God understood. I knew that He had hands to lift and to carry when the going becomes treacherous. And while I would not blame Him for every change that comes, for every bad as well as good decision about human affairs, I knew He was not absent from whatever was happening.

Somehow, in some way, for those who were looking for it, His will would be done. I tried to console myself with that thought, for today I felt completely directionless. I had no eyes to see the wisdom of this change. It seemed a complete taking apart of all the teamwork and coordination we had forged through so many months of struggle and hard work.

But my complaint, or the sentiments of others, would not change what was happening now. Someone beyond our appeal had another better idea for each one of us, and the decision was accomplished.

"Lord," I prayed, "let us find the meaning of it. More than anything else, may life continue to make sense for us."

I feared the loss of meaning and purpose most of all. A person could take many things from me, but I could not spare my sense of direction. I needed my belief that all the turns of life had importance in God's sight and that every step was a step closer to His kingdom—a step closer to what He was calling us to become.

"Good times, hard times, vacant times; let them all be a way to bring about Your purposes," I prayed.

I may not understand God's purposes in this change yet, but I had to believe they were there. Somehow, through my hanging on with prayer and trust in a God who does all things well, this, too, was under His greater control.

". . . I will never leave thee, nor forsake thee," God said in

Hebrews 13:5. More than that, I remembered the words of Paul, that he was sometimes "... perplexed, but not in despair" (2 Corinthians 4:8). That even deaths—deaths of all kinds—were a means to life in some new way.

*This is only an office,* I said to myself. *It's not the mission field. This is not the first century. I'm not Paul facing the lions.*

But it felt just as vital to me, because it was my life, the only one I have.

And I was comforted, because I knew that the Gospel was a message for all times and places, and that today's time and place were a part of that eternal message.

For we walk by faith, not by sight.

2 Corinthians 5:7

Where Are You, God?

# 30  Moving Day🌿

Kathy was the first one to leave us. It happened very fast. Even though we had been anticipating—even dreading—the change for days, suddenly it was upon us.

Monday, Kathy was in her office, cheerily talking on the telephone to clients. The next day, it seemed, her boxes were packed, her files and desk drawers empty, and on Thursday she was saying good-bye.

I realized the swiftness of it when I went to use her telephone because my office was being renovated for the next occupant. With all the banging, I couldn't hear very well.

Kathy was upstairs having an "exit interview," as we called it, with the president. Since her office was empty, I sat at her desk and, needing a phone book, began to search through her drawers for it. Empty, all of them—the side drawers, top drawers—not even a pencil.

I turned to look at her files, imagining them empty, too. The records she was taking with her were neatly bundled and sitting on top of the cabinet. Kathy was all but gone.

I felt the emptiness of the small office. I saw the nails on the walls, where the pictures had hung—birds and animals in bright-colored frames. The plants were gone, too. She was merely occupying this space until Friday.

As I had sat in my own space, clear across the office from

hers, I had not realized how complete her departure already was. She had wasted no time.

On Monday, when I came to work, there would be no more Kathy. And the rest of us would say good morning, and exchange weekend news, and try to go on.

It's funny what happens to us when someone leaves. We think we can't go on. Whether the person is close to us, or an office colleague whom we never see during leisure hours, we come to depend on them in little ways—in a lot of ways. We know who will answer which telephone calls; who will do which portion of the work; who will do the first part and who will do the last part of any major project. Without having to spell it out for one another, we simply know what to do and we do it. We are a team.

The team may be a strong team or a weak team, but it is a working team, and it is all we know. When it begins to fall apart, we are lost. How can we go on?

Something deep inside tells us that we will go on, that we will be all right. But this was not a day for that optimism to surface. Our sadness must have its day first. We felt the hole that a going away must leave, and we needed to acknowledge it.

*Oh, Kathy*, I thought. *How will we do without you? We expect you to be here, to make quick decisions, to take care of details we don't even have to think about. When you're in that office, we know things will somehow run smoothly. And now you are going.*

*Why?*

That is always the question when pain and uncertainty come: Why? Was this rupture necessary? Must life be interrupted, stopped, and a gaping hole left in place of our sense of purpose?

The pain engulfed me for a moment. I didn't want anything to change. I didn't want anyone to leave. I wanted things always to stay the same. It was impossible, not even logical, but I wanted it.

Kathy's boxes reminded me of all the good-byes I had

said in my life, to people I loved so much and would never see again. Every going away is a reminder of those losses. How much love and hurt can we spare this time?

"Please, Lord," I prayed, "I don't like change. I have lost so much in my life already. Please, not again."

And I cried for all the fathers, grandparents, cousins, friends, and homes I had said good-bye to through the years. In the morning, my pain would ease if I let it have its moment now and did not push it back. Tomorrow I would look at the sunshine, turn the new page on my calendar, and begin to look ahead once more.

And someday, at the end of all our working days, I would look back with gladness at every good-bye, for I would know at last the restoration of the heavenly kingdom, where there are no more tears and time stands still for joy.

> And God will wipe away every tear from their eyes; there shall be no more death, nor sorrow, nor crying . . . .
>
> *See* Revelation 21:4

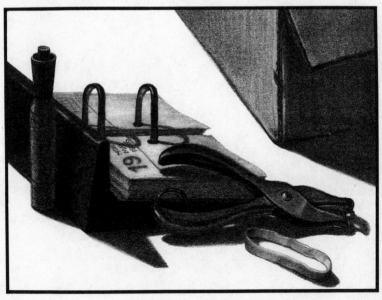

# 31

A Fresh
Start

"Look out, I'm coming in!"

It was Hal, a box of file folders in his arm, heading for Kathy's old office.

Today was the beginning of all the other moves that would take place. One by one now, we would all relocate and take up our new assignments. Whatever grief or hesitation or despair we had felt and still carried with us must be put aside.

I hoped that those of us who were most distressed had taken enough time to walk through the grief—that we had not postponed it, so it would rise up again at some other time that would be an inappropriate interruption of a busy work schedule.

Grief must have its day. And then we must go on.

Today was a going-on day.

It always surprises me how quickly people move from resisting change to acting upon it. I, who had resisted it as much as anyone, was feeling the same readiness I saw in Hal. I had not wanted to leave here. I thought the decision to reorganize was a hard blow. I resisted all the change as if it would never happen if I denied it hard enough. And now, at the sight of Hal coming through the door, I realized that I was ready.

Suddenly there is no more holding back. The tide is

flowing. The power is shifting. The "new order" is coming to be. And there is nothing else to do but to go on.

I questioned whether the new feeling of pitching in and getting on with it was a betrayal of my old feelings. No, I decided, I had simply taken all the steps in order: shock, resistance, grief, a thinking through, and now a moving forward.

When our lives are so affected that we are almost paralyzed by the impending impact of change, we must draw apart to do some hard work first. At least, I must do that. Then I can accept what is coming to be.

I didn't know if everyone had done so. Hal, for instance, tended to just let things roll on by him and keep on moving. Hal always gave the impression that anything was all right with him. He nearly made me angry with his cheerfulness. But my anger was mainly directed at myself, because I knew I could never make such a lighthearted approach function for me. I thought life was too serious. Nothing rolled off me lightly.

I learned to let Hal handle things his way. If it worked for him, fine. I certainly hoped it did. From conversations we'd had, I knew that he handled his work frustrations by putting more time into his hobbies. He was a great mechanic and a crack photographer. Both these things were fully under his control, completely unaffected by whatever happened at work.

But my work was my life in some way. Work was serious business to me. How could I spend so many hours a day at something that distressed me?

A few days before, I had taken a day to focus on that question. I had even tried fasting from supper time to supper time. I had heard that concentration could be enhanced by fasting, and I needed all the concentration I could get. It worked. I was hardly hungry. I took the lunch hour to go to a quiet place and focus my prayers.

I saw the job I would soon be doing. I imagined myself

doing it. I pictured all the good and bad aspects of it, waiting prayerfully for a picture of it to click in my mind.

And slowly, as I waited, the picture came. I saw the challenge. I saw the need to uproot myself from old patterns and habits. I saw the increased organizing I would be called upon to do. I saw my busy hands shifting papers and charts and keeping track of new things. I saw the fading of old chains of command and the forging of new ones.

I saw myself taking up the challenge as if it were the best thing in the world for me.

I felt the old job begin to fall away from me. I felt myself stepping out and onward. I realized that the grief I had felt was behind me now and that I was straining ahead to the new.

"Thank You, Lord," I prayed, "for new opportunities. For new ways to stretch. For other ways to serve. I am ready. Today I am finally ready.

"I am talking about an office, not a mission field. But it is my place—the location You have placed me for this portion of my life. And so I must answer, just as that ancient king who saw a winged creature of God come toward him seeking someone to do the works of God, here am I, Lord. Send me."

As I echoed the Old Testament words *send me*, all my objections fell away. I wanted more than anything to be useful to God's purposes. And if somehow this change was part of God's arrangement for me, then I would go forward with it.

I had not seen God fail me yet. I believed He did not waste lives that were offered to Him. So I offered mine once more, trusting that this change was fully known to Him.

I waited silently to see if God Himself would raise objections in my mind. I was willing to fight, to say no, to even seek another job if He did not offer me peace about this one. I told Him I would open any door I believed He was asking me to open. As I said the words, I realized they were exactly what He was waiting to hear from me.

And so His answer came: "This is the door. Walk through this one."

After that I could not hold back any longer. I was ready to go back to the office and pack.

... And make straight paths for your feet, so that what is lame may not be dislocated, but rather be healed.

Hebrews 12:13 NKJV

Where Are You, God?

# 32

## Good-bye— Hello! ✍

"Good-bye, Hal."

I didn't want to say it. But now that he had arrived across the office from me and was settling in, it was time to vacate my office and make room for someone else, while I moved on.

I've never liked good-byes. They make me feel as if something very serious, final, and important has been taken away forever. It's good-bye to all the familiar patterns that say everything is all right.

Good-byes were not meant to be simple. Maybe they were meant to make us yearn for that permanence which is beyond all time—for that heavenly home where we shall all gather at the end of time—for the enduring city of God.

Were I to voice my thoughts about all this, someone would surely say, "But you're making too much of everything, Nancy."

No, I was not. To accept change is to let go of something very important. I, for one, do not yield easily. I only yield after I am reassured that, at least with God, nothing good or beautiful or fine is ever lost—that what He has given on the inside is never taken back.

Reaffirming on the inside that God's gifts are eternal, I find I can go on again. Within us—in memory, in consciousness, in prayer—everything good we have ever known and experienced stands in its permanence, beyond all change.

"I am a part of all that I have met," a poet once said. Today I understood those words. I was a part of what I was leaving, and I would always think of it in its best aspects, for those things had become a part of me. "Whatsoever is true, noble, just, pure, lovely, of good report . . . think on these things," said Paul in his letter to the Philippians. And he added, "And the God of peace shall be with you" (*see* Philippians 4:8, 9).

I began to take down the pictures from my walls, watching Hal across the way as he began hanging his.

In a while Margaret, who was new to our office, peered around the corner at me. "Oh, Nancy," she said. "With your pictures down, you seem nearly gone. This doesn't look like your place at all anymore!"

It was true. The walls were bare. Nobody lived here anymore. I glanced down at the picture frames I carried in my hands—pictures of my favorite scenes and people and my favorite sayings like "Oh, taste and see that the Lord is good."

I suddenly wanted to see how the pictures would look on my new walls in my new office. With this office now bare of personality, I wanted to resettle quickly and start over. I felt my pulse racing with a new excitement; I was at last ready to go on.

But I looked at Margaret's face. She did not feel my excitement. Her face said she saw only the emptiness and the upheaval. She was staying behind.

"Oh, Margaret," I said. "I'm sorry. I'll be back to visit." I hoped that was true. We want so much to make promises to each other.

I thought of the disciples, sent out all over the world. Did they, too, find it hard to pull off in so many directions? How did they manage the continual good-byes they must say and the constant change?

". . . We look not at the things which are seen, but at the things which are not seen . . ." Paul declared in the second letter to the Corinthians (4:18). Surely that was how they did it, keeping their eyes on the excitement of the eternal. "For the things which are seen are temporal; but the things which are not seen are eternal" (2 Corinthians 4:18). The writer to Hebrews said, "For here we have no continuing city, but we seek one to come" (Hebrews 13:14).

*That's it,* I thought. *All of us are heading out toward something unchanging and eternal. And if we know that, we can stir up the fires of excitement. Change just brings us closer.*

"Oh, Margaret," I said again. "Something good will happen to you, too. You'll see." I felt my blood stir as I said it. I was ready to go—to move on toward the next new step.

"Good-bye, Hal," I called across the office. "Call me."

"Sure I will," he said. I expected he would.

And then I began thinking how the pictures in my hand would look on the new walls upstairs, and how I would turn my desk toward the sixth-floor window, with its spectacular view, and how I would get the job done that had been offered to me.

"I'll see you, Margaret," I said. "This is not good-bye. It's hello. Everything is about to be new. Everything is always hello."

She nodded slowly. I knew she would try to believe that, too. I hoped she would soon be caught up in the excitement of her own change. For as surely as one of us changes, so everything else must change, too. For each of us, change brings a chance to begin some part of our lives over again.

For God hath not given us the spirit of fear; but of power, and of love, and of a sound mind.

2 Timothy 1:7

# 33

## Embracing the Newness🍃

$M$y new office had just been vacated by someone who would be making his own adjustments somewhere else in the company. Change is indeed a chain reaction.

As I stepped into the vacated space, I felt the nostalgia of leaving my familiar surroundings drop away. This was my new place now. I would make it visibly mine as quickly as possible, and soon it would feel like home.

I set my calendar out on the desk, then my desk set and family pictures. I began to arrange file folders, decided where to place my typewriter and word processor, and determined which side of the desk was best for the telephone.

I worked very fast, racing from one wall of the office to the other, setting things out. Soon (not soon, really, but hours later) I had everything arranged the way I wanted it.

I was anxious to finish because I had a report to write that would take a lot of concentration. I couldn't let the loose ends of moving stand in the way. Once I started a task, I wanted it finished, so I could move on to the next one. I realized that I was filled with verve and enthusiasm. The move suddenly felt like the most natural thing in the world, like a homecoming that had brought with it an opportunity for even greater challenge.

How could I have resisted it so? My resistance had been natural, of course. And I was glad I had walked through all the steps of the process, because now I felt genuinely ready for the next step, ready to plunge in and take hold of things.

I thought of the people who had heard my apprehension and had stood with me in my distress. Would they understand my sudden enthusiasm now? Would they understand this process that leads from grief to affirmation? Or would they think my feelings were fickle rather than genuine?

I couldn't help it if they failed to understand my change of spirits. I only knew that I had walked a long inner road from the last step to this one. I had done my grief work well, I was ready to plunge in. From now on, I would attempt to be positive and expectant, doing everything I knew how to make this new situation work.

If there were obstacles, I would work to overcome them. If there were struggles, I would pray through them with the confidence that comes from knowing I am in the right place for me at this time. I had asked all my questions, had dragged my feet, had waited to be sure. But all that was be-

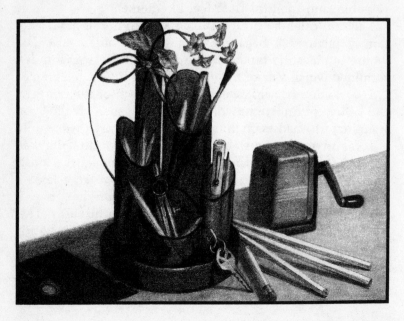

hind me now. From here on I was required to be positive, to face the challenges with a believing spirit.

The phone rang, for the first time in this new place.

"Hello. May I help you?" I said, glad the phone was ringing again and that life had gone on, carrying with it its rising momentum.

"It's me, Ducky," Hal said, using one of his favorite expressions. "You didn't think I'd forget you, did you?"

I laughed. It was the same old Hal. Whenever I heard his voice, I would know he was still there. Still a friend. "Thanks, Lord," I prayed.

"I'm sending you a client," Hal said. "Someone came in here looking for you. He's on the way upstairs right now. Are you ready for this?"

"Of course," I said. "Thanks, Hal. Don't forget me, now."

"How could I?" he said.

I laughed as we hung up.

Life goes on, and it's all right. You don't lose the good things, after all—real friendships, real caring and feeling.

I heard the elevator open and steps hurrying toward my desk. "I need some help with this advertising," said the person who sank into the chair by my desk. "Can you help me with this brochure and poster?"

"Of course," I said. I was actually very tired, and it was late in the afternoon, but it felt good to have the pace of life hurrying forward again. My mind began to think of the best way to advertise the special event my client wanted promoted. "I have an idea," I said. "Let's do it this way." I was jotting down an outline, talking enthusiastically, and listening to myself enjoying my work.

"Thank You again, Lord," I thought quickly. "This change feels good already. I'm going to like it."

> . . . I press on, that I may lay hold of that for which Christ
> Jesus has also laid hold of me.
>
> Philippians 3:12 NKJV

# 34

## Behold, I Make All Things New

Why are we so afraid to go forward?

After several days in my new situation, I began to wonder why I had felt so fearful. At the time the news of the change had come, I'd felt I was going to lose everything I had worked so hard to build up during my time in the first-floor office. It had seemed that my life's work and my hardest efforts were being spilled on the ground, as if they hardly mattered at all. And while I knew that they didn't matter to anyone else as much as they did to me, it had been hard to think that even God would cancel them out, as if they had never been and as if they meant nothing.

All along, as I held the old job, I had felt supported in my work by an unseen hand, by the knowledge that God was vitally interested in my well-being. Why then, in a brief moment of decision, had it all seemed swept away?

I saw now that nothing had really been lost. I had carried forward with me everything I had learned in the old post. Already I had begun to apply my skills in new ways.

What had felt at first like loss had now become a chance to grow. The contrast between the job I had so resisted leaving and this one was the difference between standing still and moving ahead into risk and creative involvement.

*It's funny,* I thought, *we just don't know what's best for us. We just don't have eyes to see ahead.*

I'm not a fatalist, by any means; I'm not willing to take whatever comes without analysis. But I had to believe that through the confirming prayer in which I had sought direction, God had steered me well. He had somehow said to me that this was the right choice, and I had believed it before I could know it through my own experience.

Surely that is what is meant by the verse, "Faith is . . . the evidence of things not seen" (Hebrews 11:1). Internal evidence that God knows all about these changes, even if I don't, had preceded the confirmation through external circumstances. It was up to me to first believe, and then He would show the way. He would indicate that my trust had not been in vain.

I thought about Hal and Margaret and Kathy, gone from here. And about others I knew of who had also been touched by our change. Would it be equally good for them?

I didn't have the answer to that question. My own office experiences had contained their fair share of down times as well as good times. I only knew today that none of those times, positive or painful, were wasted in the long run. I knew that I could function with enthusiasm and high interest because I had learned not to be afraid. I had stuck it out in all the ups and downs, with God's help, and nothing could really hurt me. Every adventure, good or bad, had its point. Because of each step in time, I would never be the same.

And because God was leading me toward final goodness and meaning, all those points along the way somehow would make sense—either today or much later on.

This was one of those rare times when it all made sense. I could not entirely tell what that sense was, only that by looking back I could see a clear progression, and that—most of all—God had been true to every promise of faithfulness.

I had, like the Psalmist, often said in my haste, ". . . All men are liars" (Psalms 116:11) and ". . . I was greatly afflicted" (Psalms 116:10). But today I had to ask instead,

"What shall I render unto the Lord for all his benefits toward me?" (Psalms 116:12.)

And my answer had to be, like the Psalmist's ancient response, the appropriate answer of thanksgiving.

I will offer to thee the sacrifice of thanksgiving . . . .
Psalms 116:17

# 35

In our search for contentment, we finally come to realize that no temporary assembly of people and activities, whether in an office or elsewhere, can satisfy our deepest longings for meaning and affirmation.

These circumstances are given us to live in, and to live through, that we might discover God's grace standing behind them. As we live and pray, the mercy of God's dealings with us and the beauty of His insights become redemptive experiences.

"One thing have I desired of the Lord," prayed the Psalmist, ". . . that I may dwell in the house of the Lord all the days of my life, to behold the beauty of the Lord . . ." (Psalms 27:4). David offered that prayer while all sorts of imperfect circumstances raged around him. He knew that the final purposes of life lay far beyond those problems, however dire they seemed or however temporarily rewarding.

The truth is that contentment comes by the day or by the hour, and not in large and final chunks of time. After more months than I could count—long enough to see even more major changes to the office—I began to rediscover what I had known all along: The office is not much different from anything else in life.

The old neighbors move away and take their noisy dog.

The new neighbors keep their dogs at home and put up a fence to obstruct the view. The next ones remove the fence, but they cut down the trees. Neither the first situation, nor the next ones, will be perfect. We pray and make our peace and trust the Lord for all the resolutions, finding His redeeming grace in each new situation, just as we always did.

Why is it such a surprise that no one, and no situation, can ever be perfect in itself? For some reason, most of us continue to expect that just around the corner waits the very best of all possible working situations.

Time and again we are challenged instead to see that the happenings of life are surprisingly close to the way Scripture describes them: challenges designed to draw us closer to God. As we see that, we loosen our confidence in anything else as a basis for final fulfillment.

The Old Testament stretches out page after page for us as reminder. Then in the New Testament, as if His followers had forgotten the lesson, Jesus reminded them again that they should ". . . seek the food which endures to eternal life . . ." (*see* John 6:27).

That doesn't mean to stop trying for the very highest and best in every detail of human endeavor. It does mean that the end we seek is something other than today's immediate reward.

It's hard to remember that, because all the popular literature on work promises that if we do certain things, we will climb higher and higher.

But for most of us, that climb must always be a small matter, compared to the call to approach every day with an attitude of expectancy. The Christian life becomes an extended adventure as people and their problems offer us sudden insights, clearer goals, and a deeper understanding of God.

I'm no longer waiting for something weeks or months from now. I'm expecting today that I will find—through the still small voice that enlivens each experience—one more reason to rejoice in God's many graces.

As I reflect on the wisdom of the Psalmist's words, I look back over the days just past with a sense of wealth:

- I'm learning to accept people as they are, without holding them to a pattern of my own making.
- I'm learning to respond to people as special in God's eyes and to see them more and more in that light.
- I'm learning to see redeeming and colorful moments in the situations of our busy office world.
- I see God's faithfulness in so many kinds of crises—faithfulness in a measure beyond what I could otherwise have known.
- I have come a little closer to what surely is God's intention for my immediate life: new skills, sharpened sensitivity to those who work beside me, and a keener sense of the heavenly presence very close at hand.
- Best of all, and because of that still small voice which is

our ever-present reminder of unending grace, I really do like to get up for work in the morning!

Finally, brethren, whatever things are true, whatever things are noble, whatever things are just, whatever things are pure. Whatever things are of good report, if there is any virtue and if there is anything praiseworthy—meditate on these things . . . and the God of peace will be with you.

Philippians 4:8, 9 NKJV